eXtremus

Penthos Press

Copyright ©2016 Eric Anderson
All rights reserved. No part of this book may be reproduced in any form, except as permitted by US copyright laws, without written permission from Penthos Press.

First published 2016 by Penthos Press.

ISBN   0-9982233-1-5
ISBN13   978-0-9982233-1-5

eXtremus

A candid account of healing
from the programming, demonic bondage
and multiple personality disorder caused
by deep level satanic ritual abuse

By Eric Anderson

Contents

Preface	vii
Foreword	ix
Introduction	xiii
Themes	xix
The Abuse	1
1. *Signs of Satanism*	3
2. *Sources of abuse*	7
3. *Satanic training regime*	12
4. *Satanic activities*	33
5. *Organized crime*	44
6. *Key Lessons*	47
7. *Summary*	48
Spiritual Healing	51
1. *Signs of Demonic Bondage*	57
2. *Preparation*	59
3. *Basic principles of spiritual warfare*	63
4. *Spiritual manifestations*	71
5. *Deliverance Methodology*	83
6. *Key Lessons*	100
7. *Summary*	102

Psychological Healing   105
    1. *Signs*   *107*
    2. *Resources*   *110*
    3. *Deprogramming*   *113*
    4. *Final stage*   *145*
    5. *Costs*   *147*
    6. *Key Lessons*   *148*
    7. *Summary*   *150*

Physical Healing   153
    1. *Signs*   *154*
    2. *Body Memories*   *155*
    3   *Multiplicity Effects*   *158*
    4. *Depression*   *160*
    5. *Preventative Measures*   *161*
    6. *Key Lessons*   *162*
    7. *Summary*   *162*

Challenges   165

Preface

Extremus is Latin for extreme, the word that best describes my wife's abuse and healing from that abuse. The uppercase letter X in eXtremus signifies the unknown and mysterious nature of abuse that is centered on satanic rituals. A key objective of this book is to share and thereby expose many of the extreme and mysterious issues surrounding my wife's abuse and describe in detail the steps required for her healing.

Foreword

People of varied backgrounds and interests will read this book. For different categories of readers, I have different messages. To the spouse of a victim of satanic ritual abuse: I have great concern for your well being and for that of your spouse. You are living in the midst of difficult and dangerous circumstances. The good news is that today, more than ever, there exist tools and resources that can enable complete healing. While I describe many of these tools in this book, I have a word of caution: Healing from abuse is very individual-specific, and the healing process described here may be different in many aspects from that of your spouse. I therefore ask you to seek out the basic healing principles in this book as well as from other sources of information and apply them cautiously and appropriately to your situation.

For the reader who is a victim of satanic ritual abuse, my message is simple. Stop! Do not read this book! The material contained within may trigger memories prematurely. Have your spouse, friend or a trained therapist read and filter this material for you.

For pastors or priests, therapists and medical professionals please note that complete healing from satanic ritual abuse requires simultaneous spiritual, psychological and physical healing. Healing in one area cannot be completely successful without healing in the other areas. Pastors or priests, if you suspect that a person suffers from ritual abuse make sure that person is getting the appropriate therapy. Therapists and medical professionals, if you suspect a client suffers from satanic ritual abuse please make sure the person is getting spiritual help from a pastor or priest. Even if you are not "religious" please recognize that there is a definite spiritual component in Satanism that needs addressing by a spiritual professional; a Christian minister or priest.

For the questioning reader: my writings are centered on personal life experiences that occurred as my wife healed from satanic ritual abuse. I record and describe these (often bizarre) events as objectively and honestly as possible even while admitting that some experiences are still beyond my interpretive ability. Where multiple interpretations of events are possible, I choose the simplest and most consistent interpretation based upon my Judeo - Christian worldview.

For the reader who is involved in Satanism and witchcraft: you are worshiping the wrong being. Jesus Christ of Nazareth went to the sacrifice, shed his blood in death and was raised from the dead by the power of God. He is the true High Priest and His sacrifice is the final sacrifice. There is no more need for the sacrifice; it is complete. Begin worshipping the correct person, Jesus Christ.

For the average Christian reader: wake up! Satan is alive and well. Agents of Satan and his demonic hordes are infiltrating our society and even our churches. This activity will not continue unchecked. God is unleashing a spiritual offensive that, I believe, will culminate in the return of the Lord Jesus Christ. The key ingredients of this offensive are the revealing of evil and the healing of its victims. I think that God is calling Christian churches and individuals for healing ministries. Accordingly, God is releasing many wonderful tools and resources necessary for this healing. Christians, acquaint yourselves with the tools and concepts of extreme healing, especially spiritual healing. Prepare yourselves to actively stand for God by helping the helpless in this unfolding struggle.

Introduction

On a sunny, warm day more than thirty years ago I stepped across a boundary from normal, everyday living into the bizarre world of satanic rituals, demonic strongholds and multiple personality disorder. As Grace and I celebrated our wedding, I could have scarcely imagined that my wife's family heritage of Satanism and witchcraft--a heritage of horrific crime, demonic possession and cult programming--would for three decades dominate our married life. As a child growing up in this environment my wife was subject to extreme, mind altering abuse. Most remarkable is that the memories of this abuse and the spiritual, psychological, and physical damage were completely hidden for the first five years of our marriage. Grace's involvement in Satanism was so secret that even she was unaware of it.

The effects of the abuse eventually began emerging and she made the courageous decision to go through the healing required to be free from Satanism and cult control. But extreme abuse requires equally extreme healing: Grace's healing required demonic exorcism, deprogramming and learning how to share her body and mind with hundreds of other personalities. The resulting daily battle for her mind and soul lasted for nearly a decade. But Grace has survived both the extreme abuse and the extreme healing. She will probably never live a "normal" life but her life is now productive and fulfilling. Most importantly, she has been freed from the incredible power and control of Satanism. I have witnessed this struggle and the transformation of my wife and have played a leading role in her healing. This book is my simple but candid account of my wife's extreme healing from extreme childhood abuse.

The book is divided into several chapters or sections: Following this introduction, the next section (Themes) provides an overview of the book and summarizes the basic themes that I have observed in Grace's abuse and in her healing. The next four chapters (The Abuse, Spiritual Healing, Psychological Healing, and Physical Healing) fill in the "scaffolding" formed by these themes with specific examples from our story. The book concludes with my challenges to the readers.

The first chapter (The Abuse) gives an overview of my wife's abusive childhood. While this abuse was mainly satanic ritual abuse (SRA), it also contained other forms of abuse, including what I refer to as normal abuse--rape, beatings, and other familiar forms of child abuse. In contrast, satanic ritual abuse results from the eruption of supernatural evil into human existence. It is an abuse so extreme that the healthy human mind is incapable of imaging it. I warn the reader that the content of this chapter will be disturbing; but understanding the severity of Grace's abuse is crucial for understanding the extreme healing methods used. I describe specific instances of abuse in this chapter while omitting any details that could identify the locations and the identities of the people involved. This is done for two reasons: 1) it is helping my wife recover from the abuse that is important and 2) the abuse occurred several decades ago and the specific identity of perpetuating persons, organizations and locations may not be relevant today.

The abuse my wife suffered was not only life-threatening (in a physical sense) but severe in its spiritual and psychological impact. The Spiritual Healing and Psychological Healing chapters describe my experience of Grace's healing from the ensuing

Introduction

spiritual and psychological damage. The description of spiritual healing concentrates on demonic bondage breaking. One of the central elements of satanic ritual is the insertion of demons into the participants, children being particular targets. The Spiritual Healing chapter describes how these demonic beings were exorcised from Grace and the repair of years of damage done to her mind and spirit.

Although often bizarre, the spiritual healing was easier than the psychological healing. A significant part of satanic training is devoted to the generation of personality disorder. The resulting personality multiplicity as well as the treatment for it is described in the Psychological Healing chapter. That chapter also describes the deprogramming efforts necessary for transferring the control of Grace's subconscious mind from the cults back to Grace, since much of the deprogramming effort was centered on the treatment for Grace's personality disorder.

The chapter entitled Physical Healing describes the effects and the healing necessary for the physical abuse that Grace suffered. The healing from physical abuse becomes much more complicated when coupled with personality disorder. The feelings of pain and the emotions associated with the abuse are stored in the personality states and, to some degree, are relived during the treatment for the multiplicity.

The final chapter (Challenges) contains a challenge for each reader. The challenge depends on the reader's involvement in the healing process for victims of extreme abuse. Each challenge is derived from my experiences in my wife's extreme healing and gives my advice for helping the unfortunate victims of satanic ritual abuse.

This account of my wife's extreme healing is meant to be more than intriguing reading. My intent is that our personal experiences will assist, and give understanding to those who are assisting victims, to those who are family and friends of victims, and to encourage those victims who are beginning the healing process.

I specifically wish to alert pastors and priests to the intricate aspects of the spiritual healing necessary for the ritually abused persons in their congregation or parish. I suspect that every large congregation or parish will contain several persons suffering from the scars of satanic ritual abuse. This book will also be useful for the medical professional and therapist. It gives the "big picture" related to persons suffering from ritual abuse. This includes the methodology and strategies of satanic cults in causing the abuse. I suspect that therapists all too often witness only the end result of the abuse without clearly understanding its origins.

For the average layperson reading this book, I simply want you to be aware of the satanic activity going on in our midst. Much of the power of the satanic cults is derived from their secrecy. Our society needs to be aware of satanic cult activities and the plight of their victims.

Most of all, I wish to encourage satanic ritual victims and their families. My wife's abuse was extreme, probably more extreme than most satanic ritual abuse. She has not only survived the abuse but she has also healed from it and is functional as an individual and member of our society. The healing has taken time, perseverance and the coordinated help from therapists, medical professionals and spiritual leaders. My wife is living proof that extreme healing from extreme abuse is possible.

Themes

As Grace's healing from the abuse progressed, I noticed certain themes emerging. These are general in nature and will be relevant for both the abuse victim and the person involved in helping abuse victims, especially those involving satanic rituals. These themes are also a summary of what follows since they comprise the key principles we learned and put into practice during Grace's healing.

The main purpose and theme of satanic rituals is communication and interaction with supernatural beings--demons or fallen angels serving Satan. The rituals established a gateway for demon-human interactions. The demons attracted by the rituals typically entered and possessed participants during the ritual. Sometimes this possession became permanent. Indeed, the permanent indwelling of demons in humans seemed to be accomplished mainly via the rituals. Based on Grace's memories, the method of attracting demons varied but was typically centered on some form of violence. Often this was a violent death, usually of a newborn baby, that either occurred during, or was celebrated at, satanic rituals.

Grace's memories of satanic ritual activities were laced with the occurrence of death, the best method of attracting demonic attention. Historians describe death as a common, unifying theme in satanic cults that otherwise vary significantly in style and venue. For example, some cults performed sophisticated rituals in lavish banquet halls while others did crude, primitive rituals in caves. In either extreme, death was frequently celebrated in some manner; so much so that the cults appeared to be worshipping death. But I suspect that human and, especially, infant death was viewed as a means of attracting demonic attention and favor. Most of these sacrifices were done with babies provided by young girls, such as Grace, who were impregnated and used as "breeders." The activities and rituals surrounding the sacrifices took grotesque forms. For example, the Satanic rituals my wife remembers were often very bloody. Blood was supplied by sacrificial victims or sometimes was simply drawn from participants using knives. The theme of death permeated satanic activities with violence and criminal actions so vile as to be repulsive in most societies. Keeping these activities secret was a major concern and effort for the satanic cults. Elaborate techniques and methods for secrecy have been developed by and are diligently practiced in the cults.

Secrecy, another key theme, is absolutely necessary for the survival of the cults. If the general public were aware of the horrendous crimes occurring during the cult rituals, I suspect that even our post-Christian society would support capital punishment. Only the merging of human depravity and demonic madness is capable of generating such cruelty, especially to children. The existence of such satanic rituals is so secret that even some of the participants are unaware of the rituals. This was certainly the case with my wife Grace. As an adult, she was completely unaware of her involvement in Satanism as a child and was utterly shocked when the evidences of this involvement began emerging. Furthermore, had we lived within driving distance of her parents I am sure that she would have participated in the rituals without my knowledge and, amazingly, without her own knowledge of her participation.

How can this be? How can a person engage in an activity without knowing about it or remembering it? Such secrecy is possible through multiple personality disorder. A single physical body can effectively "house" many personalities when this disorder occurs. Typically, each personality is completely unaware of the other personalities and their activities. This segregation of personalities is used to great advantage in the cults; especially with children where maintaining secrecy is particularly problematic. How this works is simple. Before a ritual activity a cult member "calls out" a particular personality in the intended participant. That personality participates in the ritual and, once the ritual is complete, disappears back into the subconscious mind of the participant. Rituals almost always occur during the night time. In the morning, the daytime personality of the participant awakes feeling tired but having no recollection of the night time ritual activities. The only evidence of these activities is a tiredness that is attributed to a poor night's sleep. This personality disorder tool used by the cults is generated by a training regime for children. For my wife, this training started in infancy and progressed throughout her childhood and adolescence. I will describe in more detail this multiplicity training or cult programming and the secrecy it enables in "The Abuse" chapter.

There are a variety of lesser themes in Satanism. One involves the opposite of a win-win scenario, common in business terminology. In a win-win business transaction between two parties, both parties gain some benefit or financial gain in the transaction. I think that this win-win scenario concept can also be applied to individuals and their decisions. Satanic cults reverse this strategy into a lose-lose scenario so that regardless of the decision made it is detrimental to the individual. Often my wife, as a child, was faced with decisions that involved abuse regardless of the decision. It was simply a matter of making the best choice to minimize pain. She lost regardless of the decision made. This lose–lose philosophy and way of life is a subtle but powerful theme of Satanism.

The juxtaposition of opposites is another theme of the satanic cults that I have observed as a result of my wife's healing. This juxtaposition accomplishes a key goal for the cults; neutralizing God's laws and standards. The intrinsic laws of God are so deeply "written" in our nature that they cannot be eradicated. However, these laws can be neutralized with confusion. A good example of this is cult training that mixes pleasure and its opposite, pain. As a young child my wife was subjected to sexually induced pleasure that was immediately followed by intense pain. This training caused her to confuse the opposite feelings of pleasure and pain. Once this juxtaposition of opposites is established with fundamental feelings, the resulting confusion can be extended to other more sophisticated concepts such as good and evil or right and wrong. God's laws and standards of righteousness and goodness become confused with the opposite standards of evil and debauchery.

The key themes learned during my wife's spiritual healing were: 1) the incredible power invoked when saying "in the name of Jesus Christ" and 2) the need for verbal specificity. As my wife's healing began, I quickly learned to say "in the name of Jesus Christ" as fast as I could. Throughout her healing, I depended heavily upon the spiritual power invoked when speaking this phrase because demons immediately obeyed my bondage breaking commands. This phase did not need to be shouted or emphasized. I simply would say, quietly but quickly, "in the name of Lord Jesus Christ ...." and an exorcism would be completed. Even though demonic exorcism was a "spooky" part of my wife's healing, it became the easiest part by virtue of the authority of Jesus Christ.

The other key spiritual healing theme that I found surprisingly important was verbal specificity. My verbal commands and prayers needed to be very specific. For example, I would never pray "in the name of Jesus." Instead my prayers were spoken with the phrase "in the name of Jesus Christ." This is simply because the name Jesus does not specifically identify Jesus Christ. There are thousands of people named Jesus and only one of them is

Themes

the Christ. In spiritual warfare, there is no power in the name of Jesus but there is infinite power in the name of Jesus Christ. Another example of verbal specificity was asking for the help or the presence of angels. Demons are also angels, albeit fallen ones. Accordingly, I quickly learned to always identify what type of angel I was requesting. I would ask specifically for a Holy Spirit angel.

It is important to emphasize that prayers offered out loud can also be heard and acted upon by demonic powers. If the request or prayer is vague or general it may give demons "loopholes" that they can use to their advantage. This is precisely why verbal specificity is so important in deep level spiritual warfare. The only time that I was chastised by the Holy Spirit occurred when I verbally asked for a powerful archangel and got a powerful demonic archangel instead. My request was not specific enough and I never repeated this mistake. This event is described in the Spiritual Healing chapter.

A valuable lesson that I have learned during my wife's healing process is that God delegates his authority. During the healing process I effectively became the director of God's tremendous power. For example, I would often identify and target a demon attached to a personality state of my wife and then direct its removal from this personality and, effectively, from my wife. The power to do this was clearly from God but I was given authority to direct that power. I can only recall one instance when I became a spectator to the working of God's power in removing demons. This occurred with the emergence of a boy personality state who was completely bound in a powerful demonic stronghold. Jesus Christ, manifest as a Lion, suddenly appeared and simply removed this personality from the demonic stronghold by fighting through hosts of attacking demons. This dramatic event is described in detail in the Spiritual Healing chapter.

Another important spiritual theme learned during my wife's healing was the overwhelming importance of human beings. During the dramatic rescue of the boy personality mentioned above, Jesus Christ merely slashed at the demons attacking Him as He strode quickly away from the demonic stronghold while holding the boy personality under His arm. Why didn't He simply destroy the entire demonic stronghold? He certainly had the power and ability to do this. The answer is that the boy personality, a part of my wife, was so important that the demonic stronghold, in comparison, was simply a nuisance to be ignored. My wife was much more important to God than a stronghold of demonic beings that could be removed later.

A pronounced theme of the spiritual healing process was the manifestation of supernatural beings and power. These manifestations were especially pronounced when the battle for my wife's mind was raging; the prior example illustrates the dramatic nature of this manifestation. Typical manifestations centered on the Holy Spirit and good and evil angels. The Holy Spirit manifested Himself as a man bathed in bluish, white colors. Good angels were always youthful in appearance often wearing white robes or garments. Demons manifested as ugly, bloody creatures that would fit into a gory Halloween movie. I quickly learned to use demonic manifestations as a tool for removing demons from my wife. Through demonic manifestations, I was able to identify and, thus, target demons for exorcism or spiritual binding. As a result, the control of Grace's subconscious was, over time, wrestled away from the forces of evil.

An important spiritual theme is that of "balancing." By this I mean that opposing actions or trends tend to balance out. This balancing theme exists in other realms such as in our physical universe. Here positive charges tend to balance with negative charges causing the net sum of charges to add up to zero or nearly zero. If this were not true many material objects such as our bodies would simply "fly apart." I believe that a similar principle holds in other realms. For example, in the spiritual realm there is a tendency for evil to be counterbalanced by things that we would consider good; although let me emphasize that goodness more than balances out evil. An example of this--and one that still surprises me--was Grace's family involvement with Christianity. Grace's mother has held church leadership positions for over a decade. This was a good activity and service to the local church. Yet, during the night hours she also served Satan. I do not believe that she had sinister motives in this service to her local church. I just think that she was unconsciously attempting to balance her evil deeds with activities she considered good.

Another example of this balancing theme occurred shortly after Grace's first hospitalization. During the most intense start of the healing process, we moved to an area located closer to Grace's parents, an area that was infested with much satanic activity (although at the time I did not realize this). Why did God move us into such a dangerous region? The answer was simple. Where evil abounds, God's grace and its accompanying goodness abounds more. Since God's goodness is more powerful than any evil, God wanted us in an area where my wife's healing would be maximized.

The single, dominant theme of my wife's psychological healing was deprogramming. Out of this theme "flowed" several other lesser themes. As a child, my wife was subject to very specific and, sometimes, sophisticated mind programming techniques developed by the cults. These programming efforts used psychotherapy, hypnotherapy, drug therapy and the simple but very effective application of pain to a victim. The key purpose of the programming was secrecy and the suppression of individual freedom and self control. The enabler for the programming was the formation of personality states within my wife's mind. This multiplicity enabled the compartmentalization and concealment of cult knowledge and activities in the personalities. This method of hiding information was so successful that my wife had no conscious knowledge of her childhood satanic cult involvement until the healing process had begun. In fact, I am convinced that if my wife had not gone through the healing process she would have remained active in cult activities without any knowledge of her involvement and probably without my suspicion of such involvement. This is truly a frightening prospect. Before the healing process, accessing my wife's many personalities was done mainly via code words that only cult members knew. Effectively, the executive control of my wife resided not within herself but with the cult members who knew the code words. Individual freedom and self-control had been temporarily abolished.

A major theme of the deprogramming effort quickly became accessing my wife's personalities in a controlled and safe manner in order to reverse the cult programming. Since her personality had been fractured into over a thousand "pieces," this work required constant psychotherapy, frequent hospitalization and years of effort. This work was also delicate, since a too-rapid release of information caused by accessing many personalities quickly could easily overwhelm my wife and cause other mental health issues. Some of the personalities contained suicidal traps, having been programmed to commit suicide if accessed by individuals who were not part of the cult. As a result of these difficulties and the sheer effort required in accessing multiple personalities, deprogramming became the dominant theme in our lives for many years as we struggled to help constantly emerging personalities. But the bulk of the work has been accomplished and now my wife has full control over her mind and many of the secrets of Satanism have been exposed.

Abuse typically generates strong feelings and emotions such as anger, shame and guilt. These emotions were stored primarily with my wife's multiple personalities. As a result, a major theme of her psychological healing became the "venting" of these feelings and emotions. Much of the work done by therapists was simply guiding the release of these feelings in a controlled, safe manner. This "venting" of emotions theme is closely coupled to the deprogramming mentioned above.

A final psychological healing theme is empowerment. It was important that my wife be empowered to control her own actions and thoughts. Much of her therapy was designed to do this. Never would a therapist tell my wife what to do. Instead, the therapist would get my wife to determine herself what she should do in regard to some issue. Likewise, I constantly had to refrain from problem solving; instead encouraging my wife to find her own solutions for issues she was facing. I consistently found that she did have the answers. I just needed the patience to let these answers surface from within my wife.

The key theme of Grace's physical healing was the powerful effect of Grace's mind on the functioning of her physical body. Emerging personalities would often trigger remembered pain—pain that, having lain dormant for thirty plus years in her subconscious mind, suddenly would manifest itself with full force when accessed during the healing process. Similarly, I witnessed that both Grace's appearance and her physical actions were strongly influenced by the age of the particular personality controlling her body. This seemed even to extend to the physiological level—a teenager engaging in physical activity would sometimes appear to have more energy than Grace could normally summon in her adult body. As an eight year old, Grace would assume the mannerisms of a child. All of these raised alarming questions: For example, what would happen if a child personality surfaced and accidentally took an adult dosage of medication? We were careful to prevent this from happening.

This chapter has been a summary of the major topics to follow. As you read on, it will be important to keep in mind the cautions offered at the beginning of the book. The descriptions of the abuse are graphic in places, and may be unbelievable to some readers. But the spiritual and psychological damage and subsequent healing have been a dramatic and real part of our daily lives for over twenty years.

The Abuse

Grace and I were on a short road trip with her parents. We had driven for most of the day and had reached our destination near the outskirts of a city known and celebrated for its history of witchcraft. As we neared the center of the city, I noticed occult emblems hanging like Christmas decorations above the intersections. The emblems were metal cutouts outlining the figure of a witch riding on a broomstick. They hung by wires across the street intersection and were large enough to be clearly discernable a block away. I was aghast that a city would commemorate such a horrible heritage and immediately voiced my opinion. Knowing that my mother-in-law was highly involved in the leadership of her church, I anticipated supportive remarks from her or her husband. Instead an awkward silence ensued. Puzzled, I remained silent as we continued traveling through the streets to our hotel. But I remembered this incident and now realize that this was one of the first signs of a family heritage of Satanism and witchcraft. This was the heritage that I had married into and a heritage that I would battle with to save the life and mind of my wife.

Slowly and painfully, the fragmented memories of an abusive childhood have emerged from my wife. Enough memories have now surfaced to piece together a general perspective of abuse perpetuated by not only satanic cults but also by organized crime. The sheer magnitude of these abuses is staggering. Yet with God's intervention and Grace's determination, extreme healing methods have allowed her to not only survive the abuse but heal from the trauma; Grace is now a functional adult. The story of this remarkable healing process begins with the truth of what happened to her as a child. This chapter describes the abuse Grace experienced from her birth into her teenage years.

Grace's childhood abuse stemmed from her immediate family and their participation in a variety of organizations. These organizations varied tremendously in intent, purpose and implementation of evil. But common to all this activity was a shroud of secrecy obscuring any obvious signs of criminal and abusive activity. Sections one and two of this chapter describe these signs and sources of abuse, including who committed the abuse, where the abuse took place and when the abuse occurred. The third and fourth sections of this chapter describe what her abuse was and how it was accomplished. More specifically, some subsections organize the description of her abuse according to the purpose of that abuse. For example, satanic cults had a specific training regime designed to cause personality disorder. This training regime was based on physical abuse and "brain washing" or programming techniques. A subsection describes this programming and training regime. A description of the ritual activities is given in another subsection. I warn the reader that this material may and should be bothersome. The bloody nature of the satanic ritual was certainly offensive to me as Grace's memories began revealing these horrid details. Nevertheless, I deem some exposure to these gory details essential for understanding the extreme healing methods Grace has needed which are described in the remaining chapters. Section five describes other abuse Grace suffered that was not overtly satanic in origin but rather via organized crime. The final two sections essentially "wrap up" the chapter with a summary and a listing of my key learnings based on listening to the memories of my wife's childhood abuse.

1. Signs of Satanism

Grace was born into a family steeped in the satanic tradition. Her parents and grandparents were actively involved in multiple satanic cults; I suspect that other relatives were also involved. Although with hindsight there were some subtle signs (such as the neutral response to the witchcraft emblems), I was completely unaware of occult activity in Grace's family until Grace's healing began.

Throughout Grace's healing process, I have learned much about various occult activities and organizations. I have had glimpses into satanic kingdoms and have identified a number of occult societies, their basic function and how they interact with each other. Since Grace's health and well-being dominate my time and effort, I have only sought out the information needed for her healing. But it is my educated guess now that some lodges, secret societies and historical organizations form a basic foundation for much of Satanism. These are respected organizations whose inner circle leaders are likely involved with the occult. Thus with hindsight, a major sign of occult activity was Grace's parents' and grandparents' involvement in a major lodge. This lodge is very common throughout the United States. Several of the "founding fathers" of the United States were members of this lodge. While I have no proof that this lodge is involved with the occult, I have discerned several clues that suggest such involvement.

An ominous sign of occult activity occurred on one of my early visits to Grace's home. For reasons that I cannot remember—perhaps to retrieve something from an extra refrigerator-I entered their garage. Upon entering, I looked up and saw a dozen large jars containing human fetuses on a shelf. My mind refused to accept the significance of this observation and I just assumed that these newborns represented some scientific experiment. And to my amazement now, I just forgot about the incident. Since that event,

I have learned through Grace's memories that the practice of infant cannibalism is rampant among "deep level" Satanic groups. The Bible records instances of human sacrifice to the Canaanite gods (Baal, for example) and archeological studies also indicate this practice in several ancient societies. This is good evidence that Satan and his demons demanded human sacrifice in Biblical and ancient times. Satan has not changed and he still demands human sacrifice today, especially the sacrifice of innocent children.

I have also observed puzzling behavior in Grace's parents that I now recognize as indicators of demonic activity. For example, one day Grace and I were returning to her parent's house from a walk with the family dog. Suddenly we heard a noise like a dog's howl appearing to come from inside the house—but the dog was outside with us. In trepidation, we rushed into the house finding Grace's father in a bathroom upset about a plumbing problem. The noise had come from him. I would have expected such a problem to elicit cursing or even shouting but not howling like a dog! Another odd behavior occurred while standing next to Grace's mother in the kitchen one evening. Grace's mother simply looked over at me, opened her mouth and hissed at me for no apparent reason. In both cases, I believe that these animal-like behaviors were demonic manifestations.

There were also other behavioral issues within Grace's family that I now recognize indicated deeper problems (not necessarily Satanic). When visiting Grace's family, I remember frequent arguments that escalated into shouting matches, especially between Grace's parents. Unlike some loving families who are very vocal about disputes, there was no attempt at, or desire for, resolution in these conflicts. After the accusations and demands were voiced there were no apologies; everybody simply went their own way as if nothing had happened and no feelings had been hurt. I suspect this behavior was indicative of an environment based on self-centeredness and abuse. In both cases, there is little need for reconciliation. Relationship with others is not important to a self-centered person who relates only to his or her self. And in a severely abusive environment, hurt feelings are dissociated and ignored purely for survival.

Extreme black and white thinking, with the resulting tendency to think and speak in stark contrast, can be signs of deeper underlying issues. In Grace's family, opinions were either right or wrong with no place for a middle ground. If my opinion differed from a family member--especially Grace's father--it was assumed that I was wrong; there was no discussion. There was a right and wrong way of doing things, but rarely was there a neutral way. In Grace's family, this led to perfectionist behavior. The emphasis on doing something the right way and avoiding the wrong way often led to procrastination since the right way of doing something was often not obvious and doing nothing avoided the risk of a wrong action.

My intuition confirmed these covert signs; both of Grace's parents seemed "creepy" to me. I remember meeting Grace's mother for the first time and sensing something unusual about her. Over time this sense became focused on a subtle coarseness in her thinking patterns and actions, with little refinement or sensitivity. This observation is consistent with Grace's memories of the self-centered and crude behavior exhibited by the participants in satanic activities and rituals. Grace's father was even stranger; this was intensified by his apparent inability to make eye contact with me. (I should emphasize here that, although Grace's parents were creepy, I generally had pleasant interactions with them, but always with a subtle unease). And something was very wrong. As a result of experiences such as this, I have learned to trust my intuition more. I suspect that the intuitive process is mainly the unconscious mind working to analyze information. Such information should not be discounted but rather retrieved from the subconscious mind.

I used to think that evil was obvious and easy to identify. People causing such evil in our society must likewise be easily identifiable by overt psychotic behavior. I was partially correct; true evil is easily identified by its horrific and lewd nature, but only if one observes it. People can be psychotic and exhibit bizarre animal like behavior that is completely hidden during day-to-day activities and is only manifested in the secret setting of cult meetings and rituals. Great evil is thus carefully hidden since, if exposed, it would not be tolerated by society. Grace's immediate family members were sources of great evil. Yet other than some subtle signs of personality issues, they seemed perfectly normal

Of the signs of satanic involvement mentioned above, there was only one sign that I should have recognized and acted upon. This was seeing the jars of fetuses in the garage. Apparently this sudden onslaught of horrific information overwhelmed my judgment and rendered me unable to accept and act upon it. (There may also have been a supernatural suppression of my curiosity--by nature I am a very curious individual.) But the remaining signs were so subtle that unless I had psychological training--which I did not have--I was almost sure to miss them.

Grace's family members, especially her mother and father, seemed to be normal, indeed, outstanding citizens of the community they lived in. Yet in reality, their minds and bodies housed a monstrous evil that was manifested in horrific, unimaginable, criminal actions done in secret. Grace's parents were not the only ones participating in satanic and occult meetings. Some of these meetings were well attended and required large banquet halls to contain all the participants. Is it possible that we may be "rubbing shoulders" daily with seemingly normal people who in secret are monsters? This disturbing possibility certainly happened with me when I married into my wife's family. What are the signs of a society permeated with satanic activity? Are such signs as subtle and hidden as the signs of satanic activity in my wife's family? I suspect that the answer is yes. The power of Satanism is latent in its secrecy. Secrecy so powerful that many of its practitioners may not even be aware of their participation in satanic rituals and activities. In the next section, I will describe the activities of the people and organizations involved in this shadowy world of evil in which my wife was raised.

2. Sources of abuse

I have been amazed by the wide variety of people and organizations that abuse children. Child abuse, especially sexual abuse, was certainly rampant in the metropolitan area that Grace grew up in. Judging by the problems in our society today, the child abuse that Grace suffered continues today and may have gotten worse for other children. All of the abuse that Grace suffered stemmed in one way or another from her parents and grandparents. Both of her parents and one grandfather abused her sexually. These same people also exposed Grace to a variety of organizations that included satanic cults and organized crime; each abusing her in different ways, for different reasons and with different degrees of severity. In order to adequately describe these abuses and the people or organizations involved, I have organized the sources of abuse into categories. These categories are incest, organized crime and occult ritual abuse.

A significant portion of Grace's sexual abuse came from incest involving both parents and grandparents. This abuse occurred in Grace's home, usually in her bedroom, and in her grandparent's house. The purpose of this abuse was mostly the selfish satisfaction of sexual desire and, in her father's case, an expression of anger. The most severe such abuse came from her father. He was an emotionally withdrawn man prone to sudden, unpredictable outbursts of violence that often became sexual attacks. During many of these episodes, the father would growl acting more like an animal than a human being. His attacks were frequent and violent enough that much of Grace's healing focused on these episodes.

Grace periodically visited her grandparents as a child. Often during these visits, the grandfather would sexually abuse Grace. No siblings were allowed to come along with Grace on her visits, preventing any collaborative reporting; I suspect the grandmother knew about the activity. In Grace's recollection, the grandfather's abuse was not violent and was what I refer to as "normal" childhood sexual abuse.

Her mother's abuse was much more subtle and often occurred when a group of women visited Grace's home in the afternoons. These visits degenerated into sexual orgies during which Grace was fondled. This abuse has been difficult to overcome since it involved same sex abuse and, effectively, attacked Grace's sexual identity. The feelings evoked by this abuse eventually festered into homosexual urges that Grace successfully struggled to overcome in the early days of our marriage.

Grace's family was also involved in organized crime; mostly child prostitution and some pornography. Most of the prostitution was "run" by Grace's mother out of the home. Men would come to the house and have sex with Grace in her bedroom. Her mother and father would sometimes drive Grace to particular client's homes for the prostitution service. Occasionally, Grace did service in brothels and posed in pornographic studios more distantly located. The child prostitution activity was primarily for income, and was kept secret using mind control techniques (described later in the book).

Grace's parents and grandparents were primarily responsible for the satanic ritual abuse that Grace suffered as a child and adolescent. Extending throughout the greater metropolitan area that Grace lived in were a variety of cult groups that her parents and grandparents were active in. Not all these groups were explicitly satanic but they did engage in child abuse or, at the minimum, lewd behavior directed towards children, especially female children.

Satanic and cult rituals and gatherings were held not only in her home, but also in temples, lodges, plush resorts, large banquet halls, caves, forests and at least one Christian church. Grace's hometown contained a very active satanic group made up of people mainly from the upper echelons of society; people who were well educated and civic leaders. Not all of these rituals involved explicit Satan worship. In fact, more often other gods or goddesses--in reality demons--were worshipped. These entities included Egyptian gods, especially Ra represented by the bull. A major city near Grace's childhood home has built a twenty foot high statue on the grounds of the city hall honoring the Hindu goddess Shiva. Worship of Shiva was particularly prevalent and vile among the circles frequented by Grace's family.

Grace's family was involved with a well-known lodge—having a presence in every major city. A number of the founding fathers, presidents, and civic leaders of the United States belonged to this lodge, the membership of which is largely comprised of decent, law-abiding citizens. However, some of its rituals are lewd (to offer a charitable description) and its senior leadership is likely comprised of many Satanists. I consider this lodge to be a "feeder" organization that supports the more secret satanic societies and cults with people and resources. While I do not have objective evidence of this, several instances suggest such involvement. For example, I have seen photographs taken of the interior of a lodge building. In one such photograph, the inverted pentagram is prominently displayed as an emblem hanging on a wall. The dictionary defines an inverted pentagram as "regular, five-pointed, star-shaped figure, used as an occult symbolic figure"[1] The upside down pentagram is a prominent symbol used in Satanism. The presence of the pentagram in a lodge building suggests the association of this lodge with Satanism just as the cross in a church suggests an allegiance with Jesus Christ.

Grace's grandfather was a leader in his local lodge chapter. His frequent sexual abuse of Grace is witness to an abusive and perverse character. Grace remembers a particular ceremony that directly connects her grandfather with occult activity. This was a phallic ceremony done in the presence of a group of men. In this ceremony, Grace was required to handle the penis of her grandfather. Although not an explicit worship of Satan, this ceremony has the lewd nature so typical of occult activity.

Grace's family was also deeply involved with the more secretive and abusive cults. Some of these groups explicitly worshipped Satan, while other cults worshipped demons masquerading in the form of gods and goddesses. To understand the activities of these occult organizations, I have found it useful to categorize them into low and high level groups. Low-level groups were characterized by very brutal and coarse rituals done in caves or forests; the elegant rituals of the high level cults, in contrast, were done in private residences, plush country clubs, and banquet halls or even in ornate temples. Regardless of the setting, the rituals were horrific and frequently included human sacrifice often followed by the cannibalization of the victim or victims. The high level cults engaged in cannibalism using fine linens and silverware in ornate banquet halls while the low level groups acted more like animals in the forest or caves feeding on prey. The brutal and coarse behavior of Grace's father indicated a low-level cult background. In contrast, Grace's mother was

---

[1] The Random House College Dictionary 1979

more concerned about "properness" and elegance. Her behavior hinted at a high-level cult background. While both parents had an underlying sense of coarseness that I have found to typify satanic behavior. Grace's mother attempted to hide the coarseness with some sense of sophistication.

Another distinction between the two types of occult groups was the degree of secrecy. The high level groups tended to hold their rituals on the new moon nights when darkness was complete. The low level groups preferred having their rituals on full moon nights. Secrecy was, at least symbolically, enhanced by the complete darkness afforded by the new moon nights. In reality, I think that the high level groups tended to be more secretive. I also think that the high level groups were spiritually more powerful. The participants in the high level satanic cults tended to be the leaders and intellectual elite who wielded considerable influence on our society. The Shiva cult, for example, typified a high level in its sophisticated rituals and actions. The Shiva monument at city hall also suggests potent political power and influence.

The existence of such high and low level occult organizations has always reminded me of the beast and the prostitute described in the book of Revelation[2]; the low level cult groups are represented by the beast and the high level cults are represented by the prostitute. Both groups have distinctly different styles and modes of operation, but have the common goal of promoting evil and Satan's kingdom. Smoothing out the differences between the two occult groups for a more efficient promotion of evil must be very problematic. One solution is forcing a union of the two groups by intermarriage. I suspect that Grace's parent's marriage represented such a union. If my analogy with the beast and prostitute mentioned in Revelation is true (the beast eventually destroys the harlot), this approach is doomed to failure.

---

[2] Revelation chapter 17

Christian booksellers have an abundance of information concerning the low level satanic cults. But more of Satan's power resides in the secrecy of the higher-level groups. The following sections contain information regarding both high and low groups from the glimpses I have gathered as Grace's memories have emerged. In particular, I describe the training regimes and activities of these groups; this information has been vital for Grace's extreme healing.

3. Satanic training regime

The abuse was enabled and protected by a deliberate and focused training regime. This section describes these cult training methods and mental programming techniques. The deprogramming necessary to counter the cult programming and retrain Grace's mind are described mainly in the chapter on Psychological Healing.

The goals of the satanic training for Grace were teaching her to: 1) preserve the secrecy of the cults; 2) survive the cult rituals and 3) function in her birth-determined role within the cults. Secrecy was the first and most important reason for the training regime; the rituals must be kept secret at all costs. Maintaining occult activities secret was especially problematic for children. The trauma experienced by children required special training and programming for memory suppression. As a result, Grace's memories of the satanic activities were completely severed from her day-to-day living. The training accomplishing this was both intense and abusive.

The goal of surviving the cult rituals was crucial for any child participating in the rituals. For example, Grace remembers an occasion where she was forced to lie as still as possible while somebody ran the sharp edge of a knife along her face, neck, shoulders, and arms. In most areas, the knife was held lightly causing painful "paper cuts." In other locations the knife was pressed further into her skin drawing blood. Only by lying completely still did Grace avert a dangerous knife cut on her body. Specific "playing dead" training enabled Grace to lie as still as possible; thus minimizing pain and the danger to her body.

Grace's intended role was to be a leader, a priestess, a role that required specific and detailed knowledge of the rituals. This role required direct contact with the supernatural; preparation for this role therefore included the infusion of demons into Grace's mind and body. This was usually accomplished through her participation in rituals intended for this purpose.

Implementation of the training regime began almost at birth and was most intense in early childhood. I suspect that the knowledge of the training was passed down from parents to children through the generations. As Grace matured, the training merged with the ritual activities, essentially becoming "on the job" training. While separating the training regime from the rituals is somewhat artificial, I think that this distinction makes the overall abuse that Grace had to overcome easier to understand.

The training took forms that alternated between coarseness and sophistication. The most sophisticated aspects of the training centered on hypnosis, drug therapy and electro shock therapy. However, simple beatings were also used regularly. Regardless of the implementation, the goal of the training was mind control. Overcoming this mind control (deprogramming) forms the core of Grace's healing. Therefore, a basic knowledge of these mind control training techniques is essential for understanding Grace's extreme healing.

3.1 Internal Mind Control

Mind control (or mind programming) transfers control of a victim's mind from the individual to the cult group or other individuals in the cult. Mind control persuaded children and adults to engage in actions that, under ordinary circumstances, they would never consider. Training to accomplish this mind control focused on the destruction of individuality and caused the loss of both internal and external self-control. Internally, the mind was purposely fragmented with the operational control over key fragments residing with other cult members. Externally, the individual was bullied into submission so completely that all self-identity and control were effectively transferred to the cult group identity. In both cases, this loss of mind control was clearly manifest during cult meetings.

Our actions result from a combination of internal decisions and external circumstances. For example, I may choose to eat a snack, an action that is prompted by a hunger that triggers my internal desire; nobody else has influenced this decision. When on the job, both my particular activities and my schedule are influenced by my supervisor. I submit to this external control in exchange for a paycheck at the end of the week. In the cult environment, both external and internal control was extreme. Externally, people were bullied into submission, accepting the will of cult leaders without question; as a result they often engaged in horrific activities well beyond their individual bounds of behavior. As I witness examples of mob mentality via modern media, I am not surprised by the high degree of external control exerted over individuals in the cult environment. Fear and the natural desire to fit in can easily override one's inhibitions when in a group environment. But I am shocked at the nearly complete internal control over an individual that was revealed in Grace, a mind control so extensive that even simple day-to-day decisions were transferred from Grace to other individuals. Effectively, internal control over a one's actions and decisions were transferred from the individual to the cult.

The internal mind control began with the dissociation of certain memories from the day-to-day consciousness of the individual, burying any memory of satanic activity in the subconscious. This allowed a person to function normally during the day without the troublesome memories of the abuse suffered or witnessed during the previous night's ritual. In fact, this dissociation was so severe for Grace that even as an adult she was completely unaware of her involvement in Satanism until she went through the healing process. I strongly suspect that many if not most Satanists also exhibit this extreme dissociation. Such extreme dissociation results in an important theme of Satanism and occult activity. Satanism is so secret that even people involved in it may be unaware of their involvement. This was a truly a shocking realization for me.

For Grace, thirty years of life elapsed before she had any recollection of her involvement in witchcraft and Satanism, memories that were blocked from her conscious mind. Such secrecy was further reinforced by suicidal programming; Grace was programmed to "self destruct" upon any attempt to access her subconscious mind. The healing and deprogramming efforts depended crucially on the difficult and dangerous task of accessing the festering memories hidden in Grace's subconscious and carried by her many personalities (multiple personality disorder). Such efforts, and the danger associated with them, demanded the knowledge and professionalism of skilled and experienced therapists and psychiatrists.

I suspect that the cult leaders have conscious and functional day-to-day knowledge of their satanic activities and plans. But it is likely that, due to the strong hierarchal nature of the cults, many participants are used as pawns and, therefore, have suppressed memories. Also, young leaders in training have not fulfilled their roles and, hence, do not have the full conscious knowledge of the dark secrets. Grace fell into this last category since her intense training and birthright indicate a destiny of a high priestess role within the satanic community.

The dissociation of memories was crucial for maintaining secrecy (this was especially important for children). But the hidden memories also contained the information necessary for ritual participation and this information needed to be retrieved for ritual participation. To do this, children were taught a code word or code touch for accessing the subconscious. Anybody knowing these codes could retrieve the hidden information for the child. That information was effectively transferred from the child's sub consciousness mind to the conscious mind for use in any ritual activity. The code word or touch position remained latent waiting for activation. Without any deprogramming, such codes could be effective for the rest of that child's life, a true-life James Bond scenario. For example, Grace had several code names that activated her subconscious mind. I suspect that, during the early years of our marriage, Grace's mind could have easily been accessed by her parents using these code names. While we believe that healing and deprogramming have deactivated the code words in her subconscious, I did not take any chances; for many years I did not allow Grace to talk alone with her family members.

The cult training did not stop at the hiding and the eventual retrieval of information from children. The process produced an entirely different set of ethics and thinking pattern that, in effect, generated an entirely different person that could be hidden and retrieved on demand. This was achieved mainly through extreme dissociation training that generated the personality disorder that has been such a central part of our experience. I suspect that most

The Abuse

members of the "deep level" satanic cults have this condition, living with a single body and mind housing many different personalities. When the programming was complete, Grace's mind contained well over a thousand personalities, each with a different thinking pattern, set of values and personality characteristics. This bizarre personality disorder will be described in much more detail in the Psychological Healing chapter.

3.1.1 Multiple personality generation

The word dissociate means to sever the association of.[3] God created human beings with associative memories; dissociation has the effect of erecting a wall of separation between groups of memories. Children have a particular ability to dissociate; the satanic training regime taught them to sever memories and feelings associated with satanic rituals from their "day-to-day" consciousness. It is important to emphasize that dissociation is a God-given coping mechanism, especially for children. When confronted with potentially damaging feelings of terror and/or pain, a child can cope by dissociating the stimuli and storing these feelings inertly in the subconscious. Satanists pervert this to their advantage.

Some degree of dissociation ability exists in adults. An example is when we drive on 'autopilot', not remembering the detailed driving information along a frequently traveled route. I suspect that fire walking is another example of dissociation--the pain of walking barefoot across hot coals is diverted from the firewalker's conscious mind into the subconscious. These feelings are, in this way, stored inertly in the subconscious without experiencing any pain. At a later date the pain may be experienced in some form, if the storage capacity of the fire walker's mind overflows or another event re-associates the memory of pain.

---
[3] The Random House College Dictionary p384

Children typically have greater dissociation abilities than adults. If the traumatizing events are extremely severe, the related feelings are severed from the conscious mind so completely that separate personality states are formed to contain these feelings. This is one origin of this multiple personality disorder (MPD). Once generated, such personality states may be completely unaware of each other and may also manifest unique personality traits such as name, voice, sex, age, and world view. If the abuse is both severe and frequent, repeated dissociation may result in hundreds of personalities; the mind fragments into hundreds of pieces. Again I emphasize that dissociation is a God given coping mechanism for children. There was absolutely no way that Grace could have survived the horrors of Satanism without the dissociation of cult information and experiences into her subconscious personality states.

The training leading to personality disorder began for Grace when she was an infant. An example of this was inducing pain by pinching her heel. Grace's natural response, crying, was suppressed by a simple technique. The pain caused by the pinching was stopped only when her crying ceased; encouraged by placing a hand over her mouth. Thus, she was conditioned to suppress her feelings/crying to lessen the pain. Furthermore, this conditioning was time dependent. Only during specific time intervals was the cry/pinch technique applied. Thus, Grace was taught to suppress feelings of pain only at certain times of the day and to exhibit "normal" behavior during the rest of the day.

With increasing age, the training evolved by poking and jabbing Grace's feet and legs. Gradually the area of inflicted pain was enlarged and the suppression of pain applied to her body was extended from the foot to the entire leg. In this manner, Grace was taught the suppression of feeling over ever increasing portions of her body. The eventual goal of this process was "playing dead."

The Abuse

This is achieved when the suppression of feelings is so complete that the child's body appears lifeless; all feelings being suppressed. The child can now dissociate completely at will and his/her mind is capable of being fragmented. These fragments form the core of multiple or alter personality states. (For further information, read James Friesen's book, Uncovering the Mystery of MPD[4].)

Hypnotherapy was also used for suppressing memories. Grace's parents, especially her father, used hypnosis frequently on Grace. An example of hypnosis done outside Grace's home was uncovered during Grace's healing process. When in her second grade of school, Grace was subject to abuse so traumatizing that her behavior in school was significantly affected. To suppress this revealing behavior, Grace was taken to a professional office building by her mother. There after just two sessions with a specialist in hypnosis, all traumatizing information was suppressed. While hypnotized, the specialist "suggested" that the part of Grace's mind containing the offending information go to sleep forever. This suggestion was accompanied by the threat of life long internment and isolation in a mental institution. Grace's knees, arms, shoulders, and neck were touched and massaged during the session; a practice used in hypnotherapy to relax the body/mind. (Ironically, a vital key to Grace's initial healing was the use of hypnotherapy. Again the touching techniques were used; only this time for releasing memories not suppressing them. Hypnosis is a powerful but neutral technique that can be used for either good or evil.)

Techniques less frequently used for inducing dissociation included drug and electro therapy. Giving children drugs enabling them to cope with the trauma of surgery is a legitimate medical practice used in hospitals. However, the cults used such drugs for the purpose of dissociating the memories of ritual activities in the minds of children. Some of Grace's personalities have referred to

---

[4] Friesen, James G. Uncovering the Mystery of MPD. Wipf and Stock Publishers, 1997, San Bernardino, CA

these drugs as the "forget" medicine. This substance was taken in pill form orally or sometimes injected.

Electro shock techniques were used by the satanic cults primarily to inflict pain. Such pain opened Grace up to spiritual attack. This is discussed in the chapter on spiritual healing. However, there is some evidence that shock treatment was also used to induce memory loss.

3.1.2 Accessing multiple personalities

Inducing personality disorder was useful to the cults only if these personalities could be accessed in a controlled manner. For this purpose, many personalities were given a code word or code name; in Grace's experience, this was generally carried out through hypnotic techniques applied by her father. With the code word established, personalities could be easily accessed.

I have sometimes inadvertently called out personalities in this manner. For example, whenever I mentioned the country of Malaysia a teenaged girl personality would come forward asking me what I wanted. Even if Grace was watching the news and this country's name was mentioned, this personality would switch subconscious/conscious states with Grace and take over control of Grace's body.

By the age of five, the hypnotic mind control over Grace was well established. Personalities were accessed or called out for special duty frequently. For example, her father would call out a "hidden" personality in Grace by talking with her and using an appropriate code word or touch. Then this personality assumed operational, conscious control of Grace's body and mind while the usual Grace just "disappeared" into her subconscious mind. Later the father would tell the called out personality to go back to "sleep." The two personality states involved again exchanged conscious / subconscious states in the mind and the usual Grace regained conscious control over her mind and body. But she had no knowledge of events that transpired during this time and, indeed, did not know that any time had elapsed.

Routines often involved arousal out of slumber. After Grace was sleeping, an alternate personality would be "called out" for participation in the satanic ritual. For example, on Halloween night the children in Grace's family engaged in the usual practice of "trick or treat." After these activities they were put in bed and went to sleep only to "wake up" again for participation in the "second Halloween." The personalities were "called out" by a spoken code word or, more frequently in this case, by a specific triggering touch. (Touching Grace's back was a particular triggering action—specific combinations of musical tones and the touching of other parts of the body such as the shoulders or neck were also used to trigger or call out personalities.) The "called out" personality would awaken and take over the executive control of the mind/body. After the ritual activities that personality returned to sleep; Grace would wake up in the morning with no recollection of the night's activities.

Drugs were occasionally used for mind control and to access personality states. Specific evidence for this emerged one evening as Grace and I went through our bedtime routine. Grace was having trouble communicating with me. She would hear my words but somehow was not understanding or remembering them. For example, after saying my bedtime prayer out loud as usual, Grace suddenly turned to me and asked me to say my bedtime prayer. Suspecting that a new personality was interfering with Grace's ability to communicate, I asked to speak with any new personalities. Immediately, somebody new was "out" or conscious asking for the medicine used for waking her up. This new personality named this drug and said that it woke her up and put her to sleep. The drug was evidently a liquid that she swallowed and was usually administered by her mother.

3.1.3 Effectiveness and results

The effectiveness of these mind control techniques was remarkable; well before the age of ten, the abuse was severe to the point of threatening Grace's life. Yet all feelings and memories of the trauma were suppressed to a degree that Grace herself was oblivious to the abuse. Even pregnancies and baby deliveries were occurring to Grace that went unnoticed by friends, teachers, and, incredibly, by Grace herself.

With the basic mind control achieved, Grace was further exploited by a more advanced regime of training. Particular personalities were taught and assigned certain tasks. Some of these tasks involved child prostitution. Other personalities were trained specifically in the rituals and traditions of Satanism. For example, certain personalities were taught an ancient script and dialect used in the rituals and did not speak English. Other personalities were programmed to handle poisonous spiders, to perform certain cutting rituals with knives, or to engage in specific sexual acts.

Personalities were also programmed to be latent until certain triggering events occurred. For Grace, one such event was childbirth when she was a married adult. An older, teenage personality was assigned the responsibility, upon this childbirth, to pass on the satanic traditions and to draw Grace back into active cult participation if needed. Fortunately for us, no child was born in the first five years of our marriage. The personality assigned this responsibility within this period wisely went "asleep" avoiding the preprogrammed consequences of failure; not having a child. Although this personality was active during the early years of our marriage, I had no knowledge or suspicion of her existence. After twelve years of marriage, she reemerged to receive both help and the deprogramming she needed for healing.

3.2 Satanic mind control: external

In Grace's experience, there was a high degree of external control exerted over individuals within the cult. When bullied by the group, cult participants engaged in horrific activities to which they normally would never have agreed. Such extreme control was supported by a rigid cult hierarchy and focused training.

The hierarchy passed decisions down an authority chain that bypassed individual decision making, such that the actions of each member were controlled by their immediate superior. In turn, each member was responsible for the actions of their immediate inferior. In this scheme, everybody was told what to do; nobody thought for themselves and nobody was responsible for their own actions. Individual self-control, decision making, and responsibility were simply bypassed.

External control within a satanic cult was accomplished through training aimed at eroding individual self-control and assimilating the individual into the cult group. These methods were less sophisticated than those used for dissociation and would be familiar to a public aware of cold war brainwashing techniques. Invariably, these methods used feelings of fear, confusion, shame, and hopelessness to mold minds into conformance with cult ethics and practices. The mind of a young child is especially vulnerable to such attacks.

3.2.1 Fear

Fear is arguably the emotion most effectively used by satanic cults for controlling the individual. This emotion is especially powerful when coupled with imminent pain and danger. These two ingredients were always present in the satanic gatherings remembered by my wife. Bloody sexual violence, torture, beatings, and, often, death form the agenda in these meetings.

The fear of violence and pain was compounded further by its randomness. For example, one of Grace's personalities described in detail a "biting" orgy of adults and children. This began by playful biting on one another but escalated into hurtful, bloody biting. A young girl was chosen, apparently at random, to become the focus of the biting and was soon rendered lifeless. Whether this girl was murdered or not was unknown, but the horror of this abuse and the uncertainty of being the next biting victim clearly terrorized the personality remembering the incident.

Discipline[5] is defined as training to act in accordance of rules. Any organization requires some level of discipline from its members in observing its rules and statutes. For example, church membership requires a certain level of agreement with doctrine and adherence to biblical conduct. Learning discipline is often not a pleasant process. While visiting a basic training facility for the armed Services, I witnessed an intimidation based training regime designed to teach discipline and obedience. If a recruit needed correction, the drill sergeant would stand face to face with the recruit and, literally, shout in his face. Most people would consider this training excessive and maybe even abusive. Yet it was merely intimidating and no physical harm was done.

In contrast, satanic discipline poses imminent and, even, life threatening danger to its recipient, bypassing mere verbal intimidation in favor of immediate violence. Its effectiveness resulted from the realistic fear of painful consequences of disobedience. Grace recalls that discipline in the satanic cult often became an excuse for administering a beating.

The implementation of fear as a training tool for children was direct, simple and overwhelmingly effective. If a child did something incorrect the penalty was pain. What an effective motivator! As a young child (five or six years old) Grace attempted to flee the scene of a ceremony. Her punishment was a savage

---

[5] The Random House College Dictionary, revised edition, 1979

blow to the head with a pipe causing a discharge of blood from her right ear, dizziness, and temporary impairment of vision. (Grace's right eardrum today shows evidence of rupture.)

Another example of fear based discipline training was illustrated by the memories of a personality I call the kitchen cutting girl. This personality was triggered by my presence one evening in the kitchen where Grace was preparing an evening meal. The new personality was initially terrified of me, identifying me with her "cutting" teacher. After an hour of letting this personality express her feelings and after gaining her trust and convincing her that I was not her cutting teacher, she told me her memories. As a young girl, Grace was sent to a school where she learned how to cut bone and flesh. In a kitchen she learned to use a knife while her instructor, a man, would stand nearby with a knife in his hand. If she made a mistake, he would simply cut her with his knife. (I doubt that the mistake was repeated.) Clearly the knife in the instructor's hand was an imminent and potential danger. Grace's personalities have repeatedly expressed their fear of being beaten or hurt for making a mistake or displeasing someone. Their survival depended crucially upon their ability to follow directions, obey their superiors and to fit into the group.

I have given several examples of Grace's training that were based on her instinctive desire to avoid pain. Fear for another person's safety was also used for controlling Grace's actions. For example, in one instance Grace was forced to act against her will fearing for her mother's safety. Her mother had been tied up and beaten. Threatened with the death of her mother unless she obeyed, Grace was instructed to strike her mother. By further hurting her mother, Grace believed that she was acting to save her mother's life and, in fact, this belief was probably correct. This was a "lose – lose" situation--regardless of her choice, the outcome would be negative. In her mind, she was choosing the least damaging course of action.

Such "lose – lose" situations occurred frequently in Grace's life and were common in the satanic environment she experienced. This "lose-lose" philosophy seemed to be a basic under pinning of satanic culture. It was a subtle but powerful theme of Satanism that Grace experienced. In fact, vestiges of it are still occurring today despite the healing that Grace has gone through. Grace still has a strong tendency to place herself in lose – lose situations.

Peer pressure was greatly enforced by the fear of violence and pain. For example, one of Grace's boy personalities remembers a bloody ceremony taking place in a cave. There were perhaps twenty or thirty adults and children involved. As part of the ritual, a man was murdered. This crassness was making people sick and many were vomiting. The stench in the confined quarters of the cave was overpowering. The participants involved were reasonable, educated people who were obviously repulsed by what they were doing. Yet the ceremony continued since any single person opposing it would simply become the next victim. The fear of self-preservation was the "fabric" controlling the despicable actions of these people.

The fear of retaliation can be very controlling, especially when severe life threatening retaliation takes place. Grace, like many other girls raised in the satanic community, was used as a "breeder" for producing sacrificial babies. At the age of fifteen, Grace became a Christian through the interaction with a friend. Grace had always gone to church; church attendance is not prohibited by the cults and is encouraged since it looks good. However, "going to church on the inside" (as some of Grace's personalities described her conversion), brought harsh retaliation. Being ill because of a cyst on her ovary, Grace was brought to the community hospital for examination. She was then taken to a room where a doctor dismissed the nurse present and, with Grace's fathers help, began to manually separate Grace's womb from its inside structural/muscular support. The womb was only partially torn from its internal support since complete separation would require immediate medical attention and, therefore, would reveal the abuse. On the other hand, a partially torn womb would likely cause future miscarriages. Not being able to bear children was Grace's intended penalty for her conversion. The next day, doctors who removed a damaged ovary were puzzled by the massive extent of internal bleeding in her abdomen.

3.2.2 Confusion

There exists a natural law in humans, a basic sense of right and wrong that must be neutralized before an individual can fully participate in Satanism. Not surprisingly, Satanists have a training regime designed to overwhelm and pervert this natural law within children. This regime relies, in large part, upon confusion to weaken natural defenses and instincts. Once the mind is confused, it can be reprogrammed with satanic morals that contradict those of Christianity.

A clear and hideous example of such training involves sexual feelings. As a youngster, Grace was subject to sexual stimulation by older women; at the moment of pleasure, pain was inflicted. The chief goal of this abuse was to produce confusion at a fundamental level. Pleasure was associated with pain and the distinction between these opposites became confused and blurred. As a result, Grace became acclimatized with the juxtaposition of opposites. As this training continued, Grace became increasingly unable to differentiate opposite sensations and behaviors. Very skillfully, Satan's "opposites" were being placed on an equal footing with God's principles. The ultimate goal of this training was to render Grace unable to distinguish between two sets of opposite principles. This desensitized Grace to the horrors that her God-given conscience would otherwise reject.

Coupled with personality disorder, I believe that the juxtaposition of opposites allows Satanists to function well in society while living by opposing and mutually exclusive world-views simultaneously. For example, Grace's mother was active in church and community events. Simultaneously with this beneficial contribution to society, she actively promoted and participated in child prostitution and satanic cannibalism. Opposites had become so confused in her mind that she could participate in these very opposite activities and still function normally as an adult! In a bizarre way, the opposites in her life appeared to balance out and give her some emotional and intellectual stability. So I suspect that many Satanists are also active in local churches and charitable organizations; the good deeds done balancing out the horror taking place at night in these people's lives. It could well be that without the balancing of opposites; Satanists would become emotionally unstable and, hence, be identifiable by their actions.

Even without the explicit training, living in a satanic household must have been very confusing for Grace. Imagine the emotional impact on a child living with parents who during the day were generally reasonable individuals but who at night became wild, vicious beasts. The mother who prepared breakfast for Grace in the morning was the same mother who denied her dinner in the evening because a male customer was waiting for sexual servicing. Both of Grace's parents were afflicted with varying degrees of personality disorder that had the effect of Jekyll and Hyde personalities in their roles as parents, the only consistent principle in Grace's childhood being inconsistency. Confusion was the norm in this wretched family.

3.2.3 Shame and guilt

Involvement with Satanism, especially as a child, invokes tremendous shame by virtue of witnessing the despicable acts of violence committed in cult gatherings. In addition, children are subject to specific training aimed at producing shame and guilt. These feelings break down a child's self-control, making the child more susceptible to peer pressure and control by the cult group. A nonviolent example of this training was verbal denigration. Grace was often placed in the center of a circle of children who taunted her by name calling. Verbal abuse certainly occurs when children play together, but it was organized and encouraged in the satanic cult.

Such activity became violent at times. In these instances, Grace was tied up, whipped, and beaten by both adults and children while being taunted. Physical degradation was also accomplished by urinating on Grace. Such acts were very successful in inducing strong feelings of shame and low self-esteem. Indeed, several of Grace's personalities have complained bitterly about being forced to eat feces. Not surprisingly, some of these personalities have the function of vomiting. This is a skill essential for survival since feces, blood, raw flesh and even poisonous spiders were ingested in satanic cult rituals.

Shame has been particularly troublesome for Grace since, as the victim of abuse, she did nothing for which she could reasonably ask forgiveness. For example, the victim of rape struggles with the shameful feelings of being violated, despite having done nothing wrong. She or he cannot assuage or lessen these feeling by asking for forgiveness, yet the feelings of shame associated with the crime still persist. On the other hand, the perpetrator can lessen the feelings of shame and guilt by apologizing and doing restitution. If the victim does not know the perpetrator, her or his plight is even worse. This certainly was Grace's case. Many of her attackers were unknown to her and if she confronted her most frequent attacker, her father, she would simply be attacked again. One can unilaterally forgive the offender (and this has helped Grace tremendously), but at some deeper level the shame associated with the effects and memories of the abusive events lingers.

Particularly disturbing was the forced participation of children in the violence occurring during rituals. In one instance, Grace remembers children being forced to file one by one past a crying baby; delivering a hard blow to the baby's head as they passed by. This continued until the baby became still. They were then told that their blows caused the death of that baby (which was probably true). What a lifelong legacy of guilt this must have produced in these poor children! Frequently, children were also singled out for participation with adults in acts of violence often involving murder. By forcing children to participate in and assume responsibility for acts of violence, an incredible amount of shame and guilt was impressed on the children. With their involvement in crime, the children, such as Grace, effectively were bound to secrecy. Secrecy based, in part, on the fear of punishment for breaking basic laws by which our society functions. This training gave the cult tremendous leverage and control over the minds and actions of the children being raised in the satanic environment and, eventually, over the minds and actions of future cult members and leaders.

3.2.4 Hopelessness

A win-win situation is one in which the worst possible outcome of a decision or situation is still beneficial to the person concerned. In Satanism, win-win scenarios are replaced by lose-lose situations in which the best possible outcome is still harmful.

The Abuse

This is a hopeless situation for those caught in it and renders them susceptible to cult control. Grace was repeatedly put in situations where her optimum choice only minimized the pain or horror. The consequences of any decision she made were harmful.

For example, in cutting rituals participants sought temporary possession by demonic spirits. These spirits would only enter one person who was chosen at random. The demonized person would then grasp a knife and cut someone. Grace's personality containing this memory described her terror of being chosen for the possession and subsequent violence. The possession was described as "being pushed into the back of the mind." Her choices were to resist the possession or wait passively while hoping that someone else would be chosen. But if she resisted in any way, things simply got worse for her. The other participants would turn on her and make her the victim singled out for cutting. So the best course of action reducing her exposure to pain and terror was passive participation; accepting the group authority. She was in a hopeless, lose-lose situation. Passivity and acceptance of the group authority and control were the only reasonable option for her.

Lose-lose situations occurred repeatedly throughout Grace's involvement in Satanism. This continuous barrage of no win scenarios leaves the individual in a hopeless, passive stupor willing to accept the authority of others. So deep was the imprint of this training that, even as an adult thirty years old visiting her parents, going to the bathroom without her mother's approval was a major victory for Grace.

Our minds are trained as children by our experiences and parents have the most profound influence. Even in the best Christian home, this training is tainted by our sinful nature and requires continuous adjusting later in life. However, for the child brought up in Satanism the adjustment requires a complete re-orientation.

This healing process is extremely difficult and dangerous but the alternative of lifelong misery is even less attractive. Grace has chosen to heal and, with help from the triune Godhead, is living proof that Satan's power can be overcome.

3.3 Spiritual training

The main purpose of the satanic rituals has always been contact with the supernatural, often resulting in demonic possession. Human control over mind and actions are pushed aside as a demon (or demons) take control of a person's mind and body during the ritual. In Grace's recollection, such possessions were often violent and bloody. She particularly remembers a demon named Jesus that was exceptionally skilled in the painful rape of little girls. Specifically, this demon would possess a male and then use this male for the raping of a child. The name of this demon was used as a training tool promoting fear and distrust of Jesus Christ. This very effectively conditioned children to distrust the very source of Christianity, Christ himself. Grace still has difficulty when Christians pray only in the name of Jesus, neglecting the important and specific reference to Jesus Christ, the one who bore our pain.

An even more effective method of spiritual training for Grace was the insertion of spiritual guides (demons and evil spirits) into her mind and body. The intent was for these creatures to continue the training and guidance in Grace's mind for the rest of her life. It is hard for me to gauge how effective this training and guidance was but it may be one reason why Grace would often interpret scripture in hurtful ways. Bible verses meant to be helpful and comforting when read by Grace would become hurtful and condemning in her mind, transforming positives into negatives. It was not until Grace had gone through the bulk of her healing, including the removal of demonic influence and presence, that this tendency was broken. Broken, but not eradicated--I have observed that vestiges of these difficulties remain in her thinking pattern.

The insertion of demons into Grace was typically accomplished by some act of painful violence, especially sexual violence. Over the course of Grace's childhood, hundreds of these demonic spiritual guides were inserted into Grace. A significant part of her healing involved the removal or neutralization of these creatures. This process is described in the chapter entitled Spiritual Healing.

4. Satanic activities

I vividly remember when, at the very beginning of Grace's healing, her psychiatrist warned me of horrifying information coming from her as memories emerged. He was exactly right--the horror of listening to Grace's memories was often unbearable. I remember sobbing alone one Saturday, overwhelmed by the horror of Grace's childhood.

After many years of hearing similar horrific memories, I have become somewhat desensitized. I don't know whether this is good or bad; it just is. While I still sometimes feel "slimed" by the knowledge of Grace's satanic upbringing, there is little now that can leave me with surprise and shock. However, much of the information that I am about to present will be new for the reader. While this section describes horrific events, they are by no means the worst--I present them only to give the reader the background necessary for a full understanding of Grace's healing and deprogramming process. If you are a sensitive individual please skip this section. And, especially, if you suspect that you are a victim of satanic abuse skip this section. Reading it could cause harm by prematurely triggering memories.

There are two key aspects of satanic activities that the reader needs to become acquainted with in order to fully understand Grace's healing process. The first is related to the triad theme of death, blood and sex that was always present in the rituals in which Grace was forced to participate. Much deprogramming and therapy has been necessary for her recovery and healing from these three aspects of the satanic ritual. The second (less important) aspect is the times and places of the Satanic activities. Satanic rituals consistently occur at certain times of the year and, not surprisingly, Grace's hospitalizations occurred during these times. I quickly found that knowing when to expect difficulties was helpful and gave me clues for Grace's problematic behavior during these times..

4.1 Triad of death, blood and sex

Satanic activities centered on the themes of death, blood, and sex. In Grace's recollection, these themes were present in most satanic gatherings. The activities were designed to elicit the maximum fear and pain possible; concern for the individual was completely absent as long as activities did not expose the group.

4.1.1 Death

A theme of death, centered on human sacrifice, dominates Grace's recollections. In fact, death itself seemed to be the object of worship in many rituals and was a unifying factor common for the very different "brands" of occult groups and activities to which Grace was exposed. The victims were usually children; especially infants. In the economy of Satan-worship a vulnerable and innocent victim represents a more valuable sacrifice. Since children are the least protected individuals in our society their right to life

The Abuse

was more easily and secretly violated. Grace remembered many children being murdered each year as part of the ceremonies that her parents attended as active participants.

This raises a variety of legitimate questions: From where could such a large number of victims come? Why was their absence unnoticed? How can atrocities of this magnitude go on year after year unnoticed or unreported in our society? Where is the evidence of these murders? One explanation is that most of the sacrificial victims were children of children. Girls as young as seven were impregnated. Their pregnancies were carried nearly full term and were hidden with concealing clothing and obesity. By the age of twelve, Grace had given birth to several children. At home she was forced to eat large quantities of food and, as a result, was overweight enough to hide pregnancies. After each baby was carried nearly full term, labor was induced and the baby delivered. In Grace's case, the deliveries were done at home or in cult run clinics. The babies were delivered alive since human sacrifice made no sense if the victim was not alive. Officially, such births were not recorded so the deaths could not be traced.

The circumstances surrounding the delivery and subsequent killing of infants varied tremendously. Grace's most dangerous and life threatening delivery occurred when she was an adolescent. In this instance, her baby was literally ripped out of her womb by her father. She was then left alone, hemorrhaging blood on the bathroom floor. (Pieces of this horrible experience were stored in three separate but related personalities--integrating these personalities into Grace's consciousness and keeping Grace sane as these memories surfaced required a hospitalization.)

In most cases, the delivery of babies was usually done efficiently and in comparative safety, the babies being ceremonially consumed immediately following the delivery. For example, several of Grace's personalities remember sitting in a waiting room looking at a book showing dead baby corpses artistically arranged on fine linen as though laid out for a formal dinner. Human sacrifice in proper style was apparently important to this high level cult. Beyond the waiting room were the labor stalls. Within each stall, the girl giving birth was strapped vertically in place, with a ceremonial bowl placed beneath for the collection of body fluids and any emitted tissues. Upon delivery, the baby and the bowl containing the body fluids released during labor were immediately removed for the ceremonial preparation.

Although babies and young children were the preferred victims in cult rituals, adults were also murdered. (This occurred with far less frequency in the satanic cult activity to which Grace was exposed.) In many cases, men volunteered to be sacrificed, the goal being to obtain intimacy with death, an intimacy that was vicariously shared by participating cult members.

Intimacy with death was also achieved using drugs. In one bizarre ceremony, death was mimicked by the ingestion of respiratory suppressing drugs. Grace remembers seeing her father in such a death-like trance, simulating death so closely that his body turned blue. This adult version of "playing dead" not only simulated physical death but also showed the participant's desire to experience spiritual death (the second death referred to in the book of Revelation). Satanists are well aware of the second, spiritual death and welcome it.

Death was worshipped in ceremonies that also trained children to perpetuate and carry out death acts. This training instilled an obsession with death in children by exposure to gruesome murders. When, as a young adolescent Grace was forced to witness the murder of her newborn baby, the dying child was placed in her hands so that Grace could feel and hear the baby's death throes. Throughout this ceremony, Grace was told that her spirit was "one" with the baby's spirit and, as a result, the

The Abuse

spirit of death entering the baby was also entering her. In another death ceremony, the blood of a murdered man was poured upon Grace. She was again told that the spirit of death incurred by this ceremony entered her. These experiences not only left Grace with twisted feelings about death but opened her to demonization by particularly destructive evil spirits. Repeated participation in these gruesome ceremonies wore down her desire for living and built up an obsession with death, strengthening the demonic presence. Self-destructive behavior became the standard response to stressful stimuli and suicide became a viable option. Fortunately for Grace, this death training was compartmentalized to several personalities and, as a result, the effects of the training were muted. However, self-destructive behavior and suicide were the key obstructions in Grace's healing process and always a major concern of mine and therapists.

Grace's experiences with death as described above have left her with deep psychological, spiritual and physical scars. Even after a decade of healing, Grace still struggles with the issues caused by ritual deaths and will probably struggle with them for the remainder of her life. These issues are centered on guilt and grief. From early childhood Grace bore responsibility and guilt for the violent ritual actions forced upon her by adults. Being purposefully placed into violent ritual scenarios only compounded the guilt. Freedom from this deceitful guilt has required spiritual and psychological healing (described in later chapters).

The murder of her babies also left Grace with an unrequited grief—grief that could scarcely be understood by an adolescent even if given the opportunity. Any healthy expression of emotions was thoroughly suppressed in the cult environment and in her immediate family. This grief was completely suppressed in her subconscious, only to emerge decades later as new personalities surfaced. Every personality bearing these scarring memories of ritual death required therapy, a process that has been both lengthy and intense.

Grace also has physical scars. Several years ago, after a miscarriage, Grace underwent a routine medical procedure to ensure future reproductive health. After the procedure, the attending physician sat down with Grace and told her that he had never seen so much scarring in a womb. In hindsight, this is not surprising--the abuse Grace suffered in childbirth had left scars that will never be fully healed in this lifetime.

The spiritual damage caused by her participation in death rituals has required a separate but equally intense healing effort (covered in detail in the Spiritual Healing chapter). Simply put, Grace's exposure to death also exposed her to supernatural evil; only a God-given means of spiritual healing could begin to remove the demons.

4.1.2 Blood

The copious loss of blood leads to death; since death is a theme of Satan-worship it should come as no surprise that the Satanists Grace encountered were obsessed with blood--especially by the loss of blood. The source of the blood was typically from murder victims or women. Victims put to death were often decapitated to capture all their blood. At other times blood was obtained from the participants, often the menstrual blood of women and girls. Blood was also extracted from women by violent sexual intercourse or via the use of special cutting instruments inserted into the vagina. (Such wounds could be concealed and would eventually heal without visible scarring).

The blood collected was then used in a variety of ways. For example, it was often smeared over the body. Grace's personalities remember instances of orgies involving the naked, blood-smeared bodies of children and adults dancing wildly. Blood was also used for cosmetic purposes, being applied to the face of women as a moisturizer. Infants were sometimes baptized by immersion in a bath of hot blood. To counteract any scalding effects the newborn was, subsequently, immersed in cold water. Blood was constantly consumed in ceremonies. A Satanic culinary delicacy was spiders dipped in blood, especially the plump bodies of black widow spiders. Also, Grace remembered a banquet with hundreds of people present being served beverages containing blood from infants recently sacrificed. This special banquet occurred every several years.

Other methods of acquiring blood included using artificial fangs pressed into the incisor teeth to inflict small puncture wounds. The blood from these wounds, usually inflicted on the neck, was then sucked up for consumption. This technique was used by a vampire cult. In other groups, sharp knives or claws from a bird of prey were used to inflict shallow, but painful paper like cuts over the body. The resulting bleeding was licked up. Before the cutting, the victim's body was usually marked. Lines and figures were drawn on the skin to form a guide for the knife. In Grace's recollection, victims, especially those selected for severe abuse or death, were always marked before the cutting. These cuttings occurred frequently since they inflicted much pain and terror, especially in children. The resulting wounds healed rapidly and were easily covered by long sleeved shirts and turtleneck sweaters.

Ironically, it was the most traumatic memories that opened the door to Grace's healing; memories began to first emerge when she drew pictures of blood droplets during a drawing exercise in a hospital. The memories and feelings associated with blood were so intense that they began seeping out of her subconscious before any of the therapists realized the extent of her suffering. Even after all the extreme healing, the blood related memories still prevent Grace from taking communion at church. The drinking of the wine reminds her too much of the literal drinking of blood in satanic rituals.

4.1.3 Sex

Sex is something that God intended for intimacy. The Bible uses sexual intimacy as an allegory of God's desired relationship with humans. For example, the only sign or physical mark commanded by God for the Israelites was circumcision and, in the New Testament, Christ referred to the church as His bride. Satanists also view sex as a means of obtaining spiritual intimacy. Only their interpretation is not elegant and allegorical but, instead, coarse and literal. Satan desires pain and destruction; satanic sex is therefore painful and is often a prelude to death. With Blood and Death, it completes the triad of violence.

This is one way Satan attempts to corrupt God's imprint in nature. Sex is so basic to our nature that Satan can pervert the pleasurable aspect of sex only by combining pain with an accompanying shame. Rape is satanic sex at its most extreme—the pain is intense and what might otherwise be pleasure is swallowed up in shame. The chief victims are often young girls, for whom the pain and bleeding are magnified by a mismatch in genital size. Gang rape was common. Some of Grace's personalities reported a memory of being tied up, whipped and beaten during times of sexual abuse. Mature women willfully engage in violent sexual orgies.

The effects of these sexual experiences as a child have had a significant impact on Grace's sexuality as an adult. The most severe impact of the sexual abuse on Grace has been with her sexual identity. For example, shortly after we were married Grace went through sexual identity crises. Her sexual feelings for other women became strong and she fought to regain healthy heterosexual feelings. The turning point was her reading of Song of Songs in the Bible, in which sexual feeling is placed in the context of a God-honoring relation between husband and wife. While the most severe issues with her sexuality have been resolved, other issues remain and will likely challenge Grace for the rest of her life..

4.2 Times and places

As the healing of Grace has progressed, an immense amount of information has emerged that together reveals a loose and wide-ranging network of organized crime and Satanism. Grace's personalities have remembered places, times, and activities of cult organizations sufficiently well to indicate a well-developed network of evil existing over thirty years ago. Many of these groups have probably altered their outward appearance. But judging by the "in vogue" display of Satanic symbols on shirts, car bumpers etc., it appears that evil has only grown. Some of this information is reported in this section. However, I do not give specific names and locations identifying cult organizations in this section because: 1) I don't know this level of detail (and, frankly, don't care to), 2) such information would be over thirty years old by now and may not be relevant and 3) I have always concentrated on the healing process for Grace, and seek information only to better understand how best to help her.

The Satanic activities occurred at very specific times during the year. The calendar days depended upon the particular style of Satanism; the lower level, coarser groups tended to have their ceremonies on full moon nights, while the higher level, refined groups used the darkness of new moon nights for their activities. Special festival times of horror occurred on the solstices and equinoxes of each year and also around the April 20th timeframe.

Of course, Halloween was also a festival time. Halloween, the Winter solstice and the spring ceremony in late April have always been very troubling times for Grace--it is only after a decade of healing that she can function during these time periods. Because most of her hospitalizations occurred during these time periods, the seasonal times of her greatest abuse also became the times of her greatest healing.

The orientation of the moon was often very important. With the moon at a certain angle, specific structures within cult buildings cast shadows on walls and floors in particular patterns. These identified particular positions at which to carry out certain ceremonies. One of Grace's personalities hinted that a similar purpose was used for the stone structures at Stonehenge, the ensemble of stone structures casting shadows on the ground with the moon in certain positions. This arrangement of stone structures is duplicated in some satanic cult temples.

Most of the satanic rituals took place in Grace's home at night, usually between midnight and the early morning hours. Participants would wear black hooded robes during the candlelight ceremonies. To protect the floor and carpet from blood stains, each visiting participant brought a piece of cloth that, when fastened by Velcro to other pieces, would form a protective barrier for the floor. The bloodier rituals were done in a kitchen sink, on a designated table, in the garage or sometimes in a special hidden basement.

Although most Satanic activity at Grace's home took place at night, some activity occurred during the afternoon. For example, a lady's group would meet during the midafternoon and engage in a variety of spiritual and sexual activities often involving children. Grace was often forced to participate in oral sex acts with the older women. Sometimes a drug was administered to Grace (usually orally but occasionally by injection), rendering her semiconscious. In this vulnerable state, the women would sexually abuse Grace. Sometimes pain was administered to her genitals as part of a ritual designed to open a child up to demonization. Since her mother orchestrated much of this abuse, this trauma was especially difficult for Grace.

Rituals also occurred outside of Grace's home. These ceremonies took place in a great variety of locations including other homes, a church, caves and caverns, temples, mines, a plush country club and even a local grocery store. (After store hours, the meat department was used for satanic activity.) As an adult, Grace was plagued by an acute phobia of grocery stores. Once the memories dealing with rituals done in the butcher department emerged, this phobia was overcome.

I was especially shocked one evening when one of Grace's personalities told of bloody rituals done in Grace's home church. In this case, the participants wore red robes that concealed the spattered blood. I shudder upon wondering how many Christian churches have such satanic infiltration and actual rituals taking place on church property! Even more troubling was the realization that, in order to gain access to Grace's home church sanctuary, some church leaders must have been involved. Grace's childhood church has been dying for some time, withered in both attendance and Godly influence.

Often when meeting at different homes, specific street addresses were kept secret by a simple method. Cult members would be directed to a street or area of town on a specific night. The exact meeting location was identified by a colored outdoor light, or perhaps a porch light. The colored bulb was inserted weeks ahead of the planned meeting time to avoid any suspicious changes. Only on the announced evening would the colored "porch light" serve its purpose by guiding cult participants to the correct house.

Some Satanic activity was also associated with a woman's historical society and a Lodge. Grace's grandfather belonged to a lodge that worships Ra, an Egyptian deity, and teaches that Adonai (a title for God in the Old Testament and one ascribed to Jesus Christ by Christians), was the evil one. Grace remembers a chant "I am the Ka (spirit) of Ra" that has great significance for this lodge. Pat Robertson's book The New World Order[6] gives an excellent description of this lodge and its schemes. Grace's grandfather was a high-ranking officer of this Lodge. Outwardly this man was a dignified, politically conservative person. Inwardly, he was a child molester who would demand that Grace kiss his genitals to receive his blessing during Lodge ceremonies.

There were other peculiarities of satanic activity worth mentioning. For example, as a sign of unity Christians frequently hold hands while praying. Grace remembers a Satanic awards ceremony where, while saying Satanic vows, people at each table would also hold hands but with arms crossed in front of themselves. Another peculiarity was a warbling or oscillating cry or sound. I have heard this sound uttered by Grace several times. This sound was used to attract and invite demonic spirits during the ritual. I have also been intrigued by the variety of clothing and makeup worn by various cult group members. The typical garb consisted of a long black robe hooded in such a way to hide the face. But other clothing included hoodless black robes with black hair pieces, robes containing ornate patterns denoting rank and even red and green robes. In one case where faces were exposed, Grace remembers the women painting their faces white and wearing bright, red lipstick. Frequently, faces were decorated with a variety of markings. These included lines and figures such as spiders.

5. Organized crime

In addition to Grace's abuse caused by her family's involvement with Satanism, there was considerable abuse stemming from her family's involvement in organized crime. These activities consisted

---

[6] Robertson, Pat. The New World Order. Word Publishing, Dallas, Texas, 1991

mainly of child prostitution and some pornography. Many of the mind control techniques developed for occult activity were also utilized for the benefit of organized crime.

The key criminal activity affecting Grace was child prostitution. This was a family business with the bulk of the prostitution occurring in Grace's home. Her mother operated the business using Grace for servicing men's sexual desires. These men came directly to the house and had sexual intercourse with Grace in her own bedroom. Appointments or correspondence necessary for this business was done mainly through the U.S. mail service and by telephone. Grace was also taken to client's homes, brothels, hotels and boats by her parents and grandparents. As an adolescent, Grace more frequently "worked" in brothels and hotels.

Mind control programming and hypnotherapy techniques were used for this business. By the age of five, some of Grace's multiple personalities were accessed for the sole purpose of serving male clients. This usually occurred at night. Grace would be woken up and told to sit in a specific chair in the living room. There she was mentally and physically prepared for "work;" i.e. the appropriate multiple personality knowing how to "satisfy" men would be "called out." When her service was completed, Grace was again told to sit in "the chair." Her father, touching her knees, shoulder, and head, would tell her to forget the events just occurred and prepare for school.

As Grace matured this scheme of mind control became more sophisticated. For example in the case of brothel "duty," one multiple personality would be called out for travel to the brothel, another multiple personality for the necessary makeup and hair grooming, then yet another multiple personality for the actual "service" to the client. Upon completion of the prostitution activity, the multiple personalities involved were suppressed or put back to sleep via code words; taking all knowledge of the transpired events with them. This was done at the brothel itself. The knowledge and use of code words at the brothel suggest a direct link between Satanism and organized crime.

Grace was also taken to pornographic studios by her parents and filmed there while being forced to engage in sexual acts with men. Fortunately for Grace this form of exploitation was infrequent. Other organized sexual exploitation of Grace included bizarre dance shows. These shows were recitals by the students of a dance studio. At the end of the show, people from the audience would rush the stage, shedding all clothing and engage in sexual activity with the dancers. I have the suspicion that the tickets for these shows were expensive.

The connection of the family prostitution business to ongoing brothels is significant. However, the precise nature of this "business" relationship is unknown. Perhaps Grace's parents simply exploited Grace and their knowledge of Satanic programming techniques for gain. However, I suspect that the family relationship with brothels and pornographic studios was more sinister. For example, several of Grace's multiple personalities talk about the "blood money" collected by the grandmother. The purpose of this money was similar to the tithe given in a Christian church except that the "blood money" was gained through the exploitation of others. A point system existed so that those members unable to bring cash could accrue points through some form of malice. When collected, the grandmother would sometimes sprinkle blood over the money in a form of dedication. This suggests a hierarchy of evil doers acting together in an organized fashion to promote crime while being motivated by spiritual goals.

It is hard to "sort out" the effects of Grace's participation in criminal activity with those of her exposure to the occult. However, there are several interesting after effects of her abuse associated with child prostitution and pornography. First, her mother kept hand written records of customer visits. This information was hidden in a desk filled with other papers and letters. This desk area was purposefully kept messy and cluttered in order to conceal the important documents related with the child prostitution business. Any attempt of tidying this area was met with a stern reprimand from Grace's mother. To this day, Grace has a phobia against organizing letters and written correspondence. In fact, she becomes agitated if an area of the house where written correspondence and letters are kept becomes too organized and tidy.

A second example of the lasting effects of Grace's exposure to criminal activity is related to bright lights. Photographic studios use high luminence lighting for the photography done. Undoubtedly, Grace was exposed to similar bright lighting conditions at pornographic studios. This unfortunate experience has developed into a phobia of bright lights, especially strobing bright lights. As a result, Grace fears going in for an eye exam more than going to the dentist for tooth decay removal. She has no tolerance for bright lighting conditions whether such conditions are occurring during an eye examination or whether the kitchen lights at home are on and too bright.

6. Key Lessons

During the course of my wife's extreme healing process, I have heard staggering details of abuse. These details taught me important lessons about the reality and extent of Grace's abuse. First, I learned that horrific, demonic evil resides in seemingly normal people. Although admittedly a little eccentric at times, Grace's parents functioned well in society, were leaders in their community and could be counted on to help with nonprofit community and church events. Yet during the night they willingly participated in cannibalism and horrific criminal behavior. Such "Jekyll and Hyde behavior" destroyed my long-standing belief that I would be able to discern evil in a person by outward observation.

The second disturbing lesson I learned was the incredible secrecy of evil. Satanic activities are so secret that many of the people participating in these activities do not know of their participation. It is truly as if the right hand does not know what the left hand is doing. Such cult secrecy and the latent evil resident in cult members were made possible by the "brain washing" and personality training given to members, mainly children, of the cults.

I have also learned that there exists a loosely knit network of evil in our society. This network consists of organizations with allegiance to varying entities such as Satan, or demons masquerading as some god or goddess. The theme that binds them all together is a preoccupation with or, indeed, the worship of death. This is accomplished through human sacrifice, mostly infant sacrifice. Most, if not all, of the occult groups that Grace's family was involved with practiced human sacrifice in some form. The fact that Grace was exposed to a half a dozen to a dozen such evil organizations suggests significant interaction among these groups.

7. Summary

The evil reported in this chapter is based solely on Grace's childhood and adolescence memories. These events occurred several decades ago. Has our society improved since then? I doubt it. Based on conversations with Grace's father and other family members, I detect no desire for repentance. It is likely that the horror goes on.

Do we live in a society where atrocities are occurring in our neighborhoods? If so, how can these Satanic and criminal activities be stopped? The answer is simple. Churches must acknowledge the existence and practice of extreme evil and do something about it. God's authority flows through the church in this age and the church must wisely and prayerfully use that authority against evil. Certainly the evil can be stopped. The secrecy of evil is an admission by Satan of his lack of power to work openly. I therefore make a call to the churches for spiritual action. It is time to put on the armor of God and defend the helpless in our midst.

I hasten to add that this is a spiritual battle against demonic principalities and powers. It is not a battle against people. Grace's parents and family members were normal people during the daytime who turned into monsters at night. This astounding realization is cause both for fear and encouragement. The scary aspect is that seemingly normal people are capable of incredible horror. The encouraging aspect is that these are normal people affected by the demonic. It is the demonic that turns them into monsters because demons are monsters. If we, as Christians, focus our attention solely on people, the battle is lost. We must combat the principalities and powers that control the people—people who God loves—who are in slavery to sin.

Although Satanists allow the indwelling of demons, they may not have known anything else. Most of those involved in deep level satanic cults and organizations have been born into this life and have been brainwashed throughout their childhood and adult lives. It is only by the power of God that some of these folks, such as Grace, are able to break away from their satanic upbringing. The Christian church has the power and duty to shield those fleeing Satan. The Christian church has the authority to break the bondage of evil for people like Grace who have been enslaved by demons. The good news is that God is in the business of freeing humans from the bondage of Satan.

Spiritual Healing

*S*oon after I arrive home on a December evening, Grace begins complaining of a heartburn-like pain in her chest. Although this type of discomfort is frequently caused by her medication, I sense danger. The pain quickly intensifies, engulfing Grace in waves that leave her gasping for breath. From experience, I begin questioning her. I am trying to find out whether the pain is present pain or flashback pain (remembered pain from the past). I ask: Is anybody (one of her many personalities) sharing remembered pain? If so, please come out and talk with me. Immediately, an older boy personality emerges and begins talking. His name sounds Arabic and he admits with remorse that he feels responsible for giving the body this pain. The heartburn pain is apparently a memory of when he drank poison to simulate death. I request a Holy Spirit angel for protection over this personality. This action initiates a tremendous spiritual struggle; for I have stumbled into a powerful demonic stronghold lodged within my wife.

My request is seemingly granted as the boy personality describes the arrival and appearance of an angel who is older, balding and wearing a robe with red stripes. Knowing that Holy Spirit angels are youthful in appearance and, for Grace's benefit, never wear clothing with red colors, I ask for the Holy Spirit to come and touch this angel. The angel immediately transforms into an ugly creature and shrinks in size. It is a demon masquerading as a good angel. The demon is put into a bag for containment by the Holy Spirit and another angel appears. This angel is youthful and is dressed in white robes. The angel puts sandals on the boy personality's feet. But the sandal straps begin to wrap around his feet and spikes grow out of the sandal bottoms. Again the Holy Spirit touches the new angel. The true identity of the demon is manifest as it turns an ugly red color. The creature is put into another bag by the Holy Spirit. Briefly, Grace comes out to tell me an antidote is needed for counteracting the poison the boy personality had ingested. The poison is altering the perception of the boy so he can not distinguish between good and evil or beauty and ugliness. Grace and I both ask the Holy Spirit to administer the antidote on a spiritual level and immediately another angel appears. The boy sees the Holy Spirit touch this angel and this time the angel does not change its appearance; finally a genuine Holy Spirit angel! This angel has a very athletic build, curly brown hair and brown eyes. The angel is male in appearance and holds a shield for protecting. The antidote is administered and I begin to relax; but the battle for the deliverance of this boy personality is just beginning.

Next the scene shifts. The boy says that he is tied down in a bed at the home of Grace's parents. This is clearly a memory that this personality needs to be released from. The Holy Spirit is now visible to the boy as a person dressed in bluish/white clothing. The binding constraints on the boy personality are released by the Holy Spirit. Next the Holy Spirit begins removing the boy from the house and from the memory. A demon immediately appears to oppose the rescue. The boy personality's Holy Spirit angel slashes at the demon with a sword, subduing and stuffing the creature into a bag. Then huge red claws clutch the boy personality's legs. A huge Lion appears and joins the fray. The boy personality is startled by His ferocity. The Lion pries one, then another claw from the boy personality's legs. Holding the demon with the claws, the burning eyes of the Lion look intently into the creature. The demon's color turns from red to black. Abruptly, the demon bursts apart into ashes that are scattered by the Lion's breath. Immediately another force starts putting the ashes back together so the Lion puts the remains into a silver bag. More demons start appearing. The boy personality is placed under the Lion's right arm. The Holy Spirit positions Himself to flank the boy on the opposite side so the boy personality is between the Holy Spirit and the Lion. Bringing up

Spiritual Healing

the rear is the Holy Spirit angel. Leaving the house, the group begins a journey through a deep, dark forest. The Lion is taking long, purposeful strides while slashing at demons with His paw to clear the way. Soon the forest is cleared and the group flies through the starless sky. Suddenly the boy exclaims to me: 'The Lion took His head off!' Startled, I listen intently as the boy further describes how the Lion became a man with a kind face. This man has holes in His hands. With the boy personality now safe, the man with the holes in his hands—a vision of Christ--disappears. The Holy Spirit and angel continue the journey to the safe place house, an assembling area for personalities in my wife's mind. Upon arrival, the boy meets other boys and girls already there. He takes special notice of a toy train set and model airplanes. Feeling safe and secure the boy rests and the host personality, Grace, comes forward. This battle is over and I can finally relax.

This experience is one of many that illustrate the nature of the intense spiritual warfare into which I was reluctantly thrust. In some cases (like this example) I was mostly a spectator witnessing the spiritual bondage breaking by Jesus Christ (appearing as a Lion) and the Holy Spirit, along with a good angel. In this example, their actions freed a part of Grace's mind (the boy personality) from traumatic memories and demonic control. Typically, I am much more involved in such struggles. These experiences have taught me many tools needed for intense spiritual warfare. This chapter describes these tools—tools absolutely essential for Grace's spiritual healing.

Spiritual healing for Grace meant breaking demonic bondage and replacing demonic presence with God's presence. Most of Grace's personalities were influenced (and sometimes controlled by) demons and evil spirits. Satanic cult rituals and procedures enabled the attachment of specific demons to specific personalities. In my observation, most of Grace's personalities had their own "guardian demons;" the only way I found of removing these demons and breaking their bondage was through exorcism. In modern usage, the word exorcism evokes images of terrorizing experiences. While I encountered some situations where I had to face a frightening demonic manifestation, the great majority of exorcisms that I directed were straightforward. I just learned to say "in the name of Jesus Christ" very quickly. The power that this phase evokes in the spiritual realm is incredible. I will explain this in greater detail in this chapter.

Following an exorcism, I filled any spiritual "voids" in Grace with God's influence and good angels. This part of the healing process was as fun as the exorcism was unpleasant. Asking for the Holy Spirit's presence filling any spiritual voids seems simple; but, as with the case of exorcising demons, I quickly learned that there were specific things to say and specific things not to say. To my amazement, I found that my spoken words had incredible power in the spiritual realm when backed with the simple phase "in the name of Jesus Christ." But since my words, backed with God's authority, were so powerful, they had to be chosen and spoken carefully.

Good intentions were not sufficient in the intense spiritual warfare in which I found myself engaged. My spoken words had to be both precise and specific; careless words could do great damage. I still shudder when I hear some Christians praying vague spiritual warfare prayers and wonder how much damage their prayers are doing. This was a key reason why I never asked anybody else to do exorcisms for Grace. It takes the personal knowledge and authority of a spouse to pray effectively for a loved one, especially one who is in spiritual bondage. I will describe this very important topic in more detail later in this chapter.

Spiritual healing was essential for Grace for two key reasons. First, the spiritual healing prepared Grace's personalities for psychological healing. Grace's psychological healing has been accomplished, for the most part, one personality at a time: The Holy Spirit would wake up a personality who had been submerged in Grace's subconscious; then and only then could the festering memories carried by that personality be released. To do this, each such personality needed to be able to express their thoughts and emotions freely. They could not do this until the restraining demonic bondage was broken.

Second, the healing process was impeded by demonic resistance. For example in the early stages of Grace's healing, she was suffering from nightmares. (Nightmares typically occurred when remembered information was trying to surface from Grace's subconscious). Such nightmares were an unpleasant but necessary element of Grace's healing process. Some of those nightmares were active, in the sense that demons were present and causing new psychological damage as they terrorized Grace. Only the removal of the demonic presence in Grace's subconscious mind would prevent further psychological damage.

Spiritual healing took place whenever a new personality emerged. These emergences depended on several factors. First and foremost, it was the Holy Spirit who awoke new personalities. New personalities also emerged when they felt safe and in familiar surroundings, usually at home. One interesting exception sometimes occurred when I was driving with Grace on a freeway. The constant drone of the car traveling at high velocities somehow induced the emergence of new personalities. (I called this 'therapy at sixty miles an hour.') Of course, I disliked doing spiritual healing while driving. There was always an element of the unknown in the spiritual healing process and while driving I was not in a good position to deal with any unexpected actions of a new personality. Nevertheless, over the course of several years, dozens of Grace's personalities emerged and underwent basic spiritual healing while we were traveling by car on freeways.

I do not recall a preferred time of day for spiritual healing; when I was present, the emergence of a new personality could happen at any time. And, since Grace's personality had been fractured into thousands of personalities, new personalities requiring both spiritual and psychological healing were a regular occurrence for several years. Five or six new personalities emerging in a day were not unusual; each personality requiring time and attention. The healing of a single new personality typically required spending up to an hour talking with the new personality. (I fortunately had a flexible job and was able to leave work as needed--Finding the time required for such healing would have been a major issue had I been working "on the clock.")

The Holy Spirit was the primary catalyst for Grace's spiritual healing. There were several intense cases of spiritual warfare (such as the example described in the prologue) that required the additional conscious presence of Jesus Christ (manifest as a man or as the Lion of Judah). By this, I do not imply that Jesus Christ has more power or authority than the Holy Spirit but rather that the application and manifestation of his power seemed to be different. The Holy Spirit's workings were gentle and this approach was usually more appropriate for Grace's (predominantly child) personalities. However, some cases required a quick and more forceful application of Godly power. In these cases, Jesus Christ would appear and dramatically exercise His authority and power. In the midst of this warfare, Christ typically manifested Himself as the Lion of Judah. Literally, His appearance was that of a lion complete with a mane and paws. C. S. Lewis' depiction of Christ as the lion, Aslan in the Chronicles of Narnia is of special interest to me; based on my experiences with Grace's healing, this depiction is surprisingly realistic.

Spiritual Healing

Manifestations of God the Father were quite rare. I suspect that His application of power would have simply been too overwhelming for any of Grace's personalities. However, several of Grace's personalities have reported seeing God the Father on His throne.

Angels were, by far, the most common participants. They appeared in both good and evil varieties, depending on whether they were serving God or Satan. This division was very clear; I called the good angels Holy Spirit angels, while the bad angels were demons. Grace has thousands of personalities; each personality was typically controlled by at least one demon. Simple math shows that she was infested with thousands of demons (a legion). Most of these creatures have been removed and replaced with Holy Spirit angels. So now Grace is filled with a legion of good, Holy Spirit angels.

The remaining participants in Grace's spiritual healing were myself, pastors and a select number of friends. As already indicated, I managed all of the deep level spiritual warfare. But I was constantly "backed up" with the prayers of a half of dozen to a dozen people during the most intense part of the healing. This spiritual covering, especially by a pastor, was very important.

1. Signs of Demonic Bondage

The New Testament records dramatic signs of demonic possession; many of them include self-destructive and violent behavior. Examples include a boy who would throw himself into water or fire[7] and a man living naked in a graveyard who was so violent that even chains were not strong enough to subdue him.[8] But there are also instances in the New Testament where it is simply stated that evil spirits were driven out of people[9]; the signs

---

[7] Mark 9:14-29
[8] Luke 8:26-33
[9] Mark 1:34, 9:38, Luke 4:41

are not mentioned while great emphasis is placed on the freedom and healing offered in the name of Jesus Christ.

Demonic activity within Grace has been mostly confined to the many personalities in her subconscious. There was no overt evidence of demon possession until Grace's personalities began to emerge. I can remember only one subtle early sign with Grace that gradually became more pronounced: during communion services at church she would become uncomfortable and ill, often walking out. With hindsight, it is clear that the communion service commemorating the sacrifice of Christ reminded Grace, on a subconscious level, of her involvement with the horrors of satanic rituals and demonic interaction.

I suspect that any reasonably large congregation will have several people suffering from satanic ritual abuse; pastors would be wise to be on the lookout during communion for people (especially women) that consistently step out of the service. Such behavior may be an indicator of demonic torment and could identify those needing help.

As Grace's healing process began, more explicit signs of demonic influence emerged. The first such sign occurred when Grace was hypnotized in an effort to unlock some of her memories. During this process, Grace sensed a glowing red presence in her subconscious. Red was a color that, for Grace, indicated a demonic presence. Grace's therapist wisely did not try removing the red presence but rather asked for God's presence in Grace's subconscious. Immediately, the red light was overcome by a bluish, white light—the colors of the Holy Spirit. (In Grace's experience, the presence of bluish, white light always signified the presence of the Holy Spirit.)

When Grace's personality states began emerging, several particular demonic manifestations became common. Externally, Grace's hands would often curl into a claw-like shape; internally, she might receive a sudden impulse to hurt me.

Spiritual Healing

One sign occurred when Grace and I were moving back toward her childhood home; after driving all day we had found a motel room for the night just after crossing the border into Grace's home state. The next morning I noticed that my wristwatch—a watch with no history of malfunction--had stopped exactly at midnight. Was this a coincidence? Also that night Grace had a dream in which a threatening spiritual force coming towards her was pushed away by a large "hand." I suspect that the stopped watch and the dream were harbingers of spiritual struggles about to commence as we moved back into the evil principalities of Grace's childhood.

At one point very early in the healing process, I asked Grace how many demons were in her that needed removal; she replied that there was a legion of demons within her, an answer that appeared to spontaneously come from her subconscious mind. At the time I was very puzzled and skeptical of this answer. However the number turned out to be correct and several years later, after exorcising over a thousand demons from Grace, I simply stopped counting.

I used these signs (and others like them) as an indication that direct and immediate spiritual action was needed. But without intense preparation I could never have been prepared for this battle.

2. Preparation

How does a Christian, like me, raised in an evangelical church prepare for spiritual warfare with demons and evil spirits? Over thirty years worth of sermons and Sunday school lessons had given me a solid foundation for Christian living. But my knowledge of spiritual warfare was woefully lacking. My response was to pray, fast, and seek out Christians who could explain the principles of this kind of spiritual warfare.

2.1 Personal Preparation

Early in Grace's healing, I realized the spiritual nature of her abuse and, accordingly, began preparations for the spiritual battle. Initially, this consisted of several months of concentrated prayer and fasting. Prayer is always powerful but when combined with fasting, the power of prayer is multiplied. There are several reasons for fasting mentioned in the Bible. My fasting was a combination of the Ezra Fast[10] (protection from harm) and the Jesus Fast[11] (preparation for a spiritual battle). In the Old Testament book of Ezra, he shares his concern for safety as he led a group of exiles returning to Jerusalem with many gold, silver and precious items for the House of God. He prayed and fasted, pleading for protection from harm on the journey and did receive protection during his travels. The Jesus Fast was a forty day fast in the desert in which Christ prepared for the upcoming spiritual battle with Satan.

By no means did I understand the exact nature of fasting, but I was convinced that fasting was absolutely necessary for the "heavy duty" spiritual warfare that I needed to become engaged in during Grace's healing process. Fasting had the effect of enabling my body and spirit to be a conduit for God's power. That power was unleashed against the evil resident in Grace; giving her the protection and the freedom needed for healing.

Christ fasted in the desert for forty days. My fasts have been (and still are) light fasts, usually substituting prayer for lunch. Light fasting conserved physical strength for the draining struggles that accompanied the demonic bondage breaking. As Grace's healing progressed, I modified my fasting from every week to occasional weekly fasts. These weekly fasts typically coincided with the times of high satanic activity, including Halloween, the Winter solstice, the Spring Equinox and April 20th. It had been

---
[10] Ezra 8:21-23
[11] Matthew 4:11

during these times that most of the abuse occurred; in retrospect, it has also been during these times that a great deal of Grace's healing has taken place.

My preparatory prayers were requests for wisdom, discernment, strength, and guidance. I also found it important to pray for a general binding and isolation of the demons in Grace, for the obstruction of demonic communications and for her healing to occur at the appropriate pace. These prayer themes continued throughout the healing process. Prayer for personal protection during the healing process was also essential to maintain spiritual strength in strange and potentially dangerous circumstances. Protective intercessory prayers were important for pastors, therapists, and others participating in the healing process.

This prayer was especially important in the early phases of Grace's healing. During her first hospitalization a special therapy session using a drug useful for releasing blocked information was scheduled. Several days prior to this session, the only doctor in the area qualified to administer and oversee this drug therapy was killed in an automobile accident. Was this merely a coincidence? I don't know but I do know that while we live in Satan's world we must be prepared for opposition of all kinds.

2.2 Finding a Church

I think that individual freedom occurs most often in a church not artificially bound by theology or tradition. While any good church has its particular theological teaching, customs and traditions, these should not be used to intimidate people or constrain the power of the Holy Spirit. An atmosphere of individual freedom in a church encourages openness and safety; both are essential if the barriers of guilt and shame are to be breached with healing. Accordingly, I searched for a church holding firm to basic Christian beliefs as found in the Nicene Creed but not stressing more sophisticated theology. Such a church should be open to manifestations of the Holy Spirit whatever they may be. I found that such churches often exhibited much diversity in the social makeup of the congregation and even in Sunday morning dress. I have most often found these traits in Vineyard churches; in many ways, I consider Vineyard churches to be the "special forces" in God's army. However, I am convinced that God's power for healing is ready to be poured out onto any Christian church willing to accept it.

2.3 Developing a Spiritual Warfare Team

Once a good church home was established, I sought out individuals willing to pray weekly with Grace and myself. A spiritual team complimented the medical and psychological teams established. Since Grace had been abused by spiritual groups, it was best if spiritual healing occurred in a similar group, but in a Christian setting.

Spiritual warfare must not be entered into lightly but rather with commitment and awareness. The goal of the spiritual team was to provide spiritual stability, healing and protection. We maintained stability through encouragement and by sharing Bible verses and insights. The week by week perseverance of the team members gave Grace the security of knowing somebody cared deeply for her welfare.

All members of the team were mature, dedicated Christians free from unhealed emotional and spiritual wounds. The pastor of our church was the key member of the team by virtue of his spiritual authority, since only he can provide an adequate spiritual covering for the members of the congregation. In one instance, a multiple personality trained as a high priestess asked the pastor to hold her hands and pray a blessing over them. During the prayer,

Spiritual Healing

Grace (as an internal observer) could see the personality's bloody hands being cleansed. The pastor had both the spiritual authority and the discernment to accomplish the cleansing.

The pastor's role was limited--he wisely refrained from engaging in any direct counseling with Grace. (With hindsight, I now know that conventional pastoral counseling with a victim of satanic abuse can easily back-fire, causing more damage.) Overall this team was equipped for healing: they were good listeners, patient, spiritually sensitive and slow to aggressively offer quick solutions. The world view and operational thinking of someone involved in Satanism is so warped that conventional problem solving is often not relevant or useful.

Demolishing the kind of demonic strongholds that I encountered in Grace's mind cannot be entered into lightly but requires both commitment and discernment. Grace and I owe much to the efforts and courage of these spiritual team members, a number of whom endured difficult spiritual attacks.

3. Basic principles of spiritual warfare

The spiritual universe, like the physical universe, operates according to a set of God-ordained laws. Based on my understanding of these laws and on my observations during Grace's healing, I have formulated some fundamental principles of spiritual healing.

3.1 No-fear rule and spiritual hierarchy

Fear is one of the main tools of the demonic. Early in Grace's healing process, I learned not to be terrorized or incapacitated by fear of the supernatural. I call this the no fear rule. While a complete lack of fear is unrealistic (especially when dealing with the demonic), I found it crucial not to act out of fear or to make decisions based on fear

My confidence primarily grew from a clear understanding of spiritual authority. We read in the gospels that Jesus Christ exercised this authority frequently during his earthly ministry. (It is notable that, while humans questioned the authority of Christ, demons never did.) It has been my observation that the "lines of authority" are much clearer in the spiritual realm than in our current human realm of existence. Understanding how my family and I fit into this spiritual hierarchy gave me confidence in the no fear rule for the extreme spiritual warfare required for Grace's healing.

The spiritual universe has a well-defined hierarchy of authority to which spiritual beings must submit. The Triune Godhead is first; all beings are ultimately under authority of God, through Jesus Christ and the Holy Spirit. After this come, in order: the church, angels and demons, unsaved humans and the rest of creation. Within the church, pastors have authority over their congregation. The congregation is made up of families and husbands have authority over their own family.

Satan's realm has a rigid authority structure that includes a strong geographic component. For example, demonic boundaries can coincide with state boundaries in the United States, with each state divided up into smaller regions of demonic dominance—these are the principalities. Grace and I could sense a boundary of our particular satanic principality simply while driving across it on a major highway. When crossing the boundary line, Grace sensed a noticeable spiritual attack, manifest as a sudden apprehension or illness. This particular sensitivity has lessened as her healing has progressed.

Besides the geographical division of Satan's authority, I also observed a definite ranking of demons as they were expelled from Grace. I often encountered groupings of five to six demons serving a single more powerful demon.

Unfortunately, unsaved humans are at the bottom of the spiritual hierarchy. Their main protection now is the general spiritual disconnect that God has placed between humans and supernatural beings. At Christ's second coming, I believe that this disconnect will be removed and unsaved humans will be subject to the direct horrors of the demonic.

By virtue of this spiritual hierarchy, Christians (the church) have been placed in a powerful position of authority. This authority appears solely through the death and resurrection of Jesus Christ, making possible the gift of salvation for all people. When a person accepts this gift and becomes a child of God, he or she becomes an emissary of God. God's incredible power and authority is then able to flow through this person—but only if he or she is willing to let it. This power is only directed and channeled by Christians; it is entirely God's power. This is why it is crucial to audibly say "by the power of the Lord Jesus Christ" or "in the name of the Lord Jesus Christ" when dealing with the demonic. Implementing the power of God via the statement "in the name of Jesus Christ" is a theme of this chapter.

Because of my position in the spiritual hierarchy, I had authority over any demons or evil spirits attacking my family. I used this authority on a daily basis for several years. While I still needed to use good judgment, I remain utterly amazed at how immediately my commands in the spiritual realm were obeyed by demons. It must be Satan's greatest fear that Christians would, in mass, realize and utilize this power available to us against the demonic realms. Understanding my position in the spiritual hierarchy and experiencing the spiritual power flowing through me enabled me to implement the no fear and spiritual hierarchy rules.

3.1.1 Implementation

To effectively use the spiritual authority given to Christians, I learned and honored the spiritual hierarchy established by God.

For example when demonic manifestations occurred in Grace (the details are described later), it meant my family was under attack. I therefore had both the authority and responsibility to command the manifesting demons to be bound, silenced and removed from my wife. My right to do this was backed up by the authority and power of Jesus Christ. This situation has occurred hundreds of times and never has a demonic attack persisted for more than fifteen seconds. However when exorcising demons from Grace, I was very careful to exorcise only those demons manifesting or those demons connected to a particular personality who had emerged or "woken up." I knew that hundreds of demons probably remained attached to other personalities still "sleeping." Many of these personalities were explicitly "created" by Grace's parents to be under their control—until they wake up, they may not be under either my authority or Grace's. As such, I did not wish to harm Grace by attempting to exert spiritual authority over any personality that was not yet ready to accept my authority. This strategy has been helpful both in minimizing the collateral damage to personalities not ready for healing and by slowing down the spiritual warfare to a manageable rate.

"Fitting into" the spiritual hierarchy of the Christian community means that my family is under the spiritual authority of a pastor. Understanding this principle and submitting to the pastor of our local church was crucial for Grace's healing. For example after moving across country, Grace and I began attending a church that was new to us. At the end of a Sunday morning service, an associate pastor closed the service with prayer in the name of Jesus, not Jesus Christ. (As I will discuss later, this language often makes Grace vulnerable to spiritual attack.) She immediately became physically ill and agitated. While my prayers showed some effect, the demonic attack persisted. Only when the senior pastor prayed a spiritual covering over us in the name of Jesus Christ, did the demonic attack stop.

The spiritual authority of a Christian pastor is immense. A door for evil had been inadvertently opened and I did not possess a pastor's authority to close it. By acting upon this knowledge and placing ourselves under the senior pastor's authority we were able to defeat a strong and potentially damaging demonic attack on Grace.

3.2 People First Rule

The rescue of the boy personality by the Lion, the Holy Spirit and a Holy Spirit angel was described in the prologue to this chapter. During this rescue the Lion did not destroy the opposing demons but merely "batted" them out of the way. Surely the Lion, Jesus Christ, had the power and authority to destroy any opposing demons. So why did He not simply destroy the demons and then rescue the boy? I believe the answer to this question is that Christ was concentrated on helping the boy and considered the demons a mere nuisance. This attitude illustrates the next basic principle of spiritual healing that I call the people first rule. People are so valuable to God that all attention is concentrated on humans and not on other spiritual beings. Obstructing demonic influences are simply pushed aside so that the healing can focus on the person in trouble.

Understanding the people first rule helped guide my decisions on how best to help Grace. When one of Grace's personalities woke up, demons were often exposed. Unless the demons were interfering with the psychological healing process, I temporarily ignored them. If they did interfere, I would briefly divert my attention in order to silence the demons. I tried to concentrate strictly on Grace's well-being. (By far the most difficult part of Grace's healing process was dealing with the psychological aspects of Grace's healing, especially when newly awakened personalities were processing their memories.) The spiritual side of the healing--such as dealing with the demonic--was much easier to handle once I learned and implemented the spiritual rules.

3.3 God is a gentleman

Another spiritual principle of healing was that God is a gentleman. By this I mean that he does not force His will upon us even in cases we might think it reasonable or useful. God created us with the ability to choose good or evil and does not violate this principle. Since some people are slaves to sin and choose evil, the horrendous evil Grace experienced as a child and adolescent not only exists but currently flourishes. The God is a gentleman principle means that the courtesy of freedom of choice was extended to each personality within Grace. For example, I have witnessed the Holy Spirit holding a demon passively until given permission by the personality involved to remove the creature. (Of course, Grace can give such permission but she may not be available or she may not be able to communicate with the personality involved.)

This was another reason I was cautious when exorcising demons. Personalities often valued demons as their spiritual friends and guides so I was careful in managing the deliverance. Removing a demon without trust and without consent can thwart the authority and power of the Holy Spirit that is so necessary for complete healing. If one of Grace's personalities was not ready for the removal of demons, I simply asked that the demons be bound and silenced only. While the eventual removal of demons was necessary, the binding and silencing of demons was all that was needed to neutralize demonic opposition and continue healing.

3.3.1 Spiritual teamwork

A corollary to the God is a gentleman principle is that God treats us with dignity by allowing us to participate in the healing

Spiritual Healing

process to the full extent of our capabilities. In my observation, God prefers working in partnership with us. I did my part in the healing process and God took over when my resources were exhausted and when my capabilities were exceeded. A good example of this was the removal of an unusually powerful demon from a boy personality in Grace. In this case, I had interacted with the boy for nearly an hour and had finally convinced him to go to the safe place house while targeting a half dozen demons for removal by the Holy Spirit. (The safe place house is described in detail in the next chapter.)

Even after this, I was encountering opposition. Something was preventing the arrival of a Holy Spirit angel. When this angel finally appeared, dressed in jeans and wearing hiking boots (the boy was interested in camping), blood was splattered over the Holy Spirit (who was also present). Upon striking the Holy Spirit, the blood turned into a silvery substance reflecting light. In the reflection, the boy personality could see a powerful demon and informed me of this. Immediately, I targeted this demon for removal. Next the Lion, Jesus Christ, appeared and the demon tried to flee but was caught and thrown into a vault where it was frozen. Finished with His work, the Lion went over to the Holy Spirit for discussion. The Holy Spirit by now had replaced the splattered blood with sparkling lights the boy described as stars. This example illustrates the teamwork inherent in spiritual healing on several levels. Initially it was through my efforts in talking with the boy personality that forced this chief demon into a position of manifestation, exposure, and, hence, removal. I am certain that God's power expressed through the Holy Spirit or the Lion of Judah could have removed this demon independently of me. Yet by transforming the offending blood into a mirror exposing the demon, the Holy Spirit kept me involved by giving me the opportunity of targeting this troublesome creature for removal. On another level, Jesus Christ teamed with the Holy Spirit in the removal of the demon. The Holy Spirit illuminated the demon for removal by Christ, the Lion.

3.4 Specificity

On a Sunday morning, one of Grace's 'gatekeeper' personalities woke up. (I have observed that these personalities seem to mediate between the conscious and subconscious and can access sleeping personalities.) In addition, several other personalities were waking up that morning. As I listened, one of them described a sleeping room in which personalities of all ages were sleeping in beds covered with white blankets. (This room was located in Grace's subconscious.) Grace observed several good angels protecting the room, although demons were just outside the door trying to enter. In an attempt to reinforce the Holy Spirit angels guarding this room, I verbally asked for a powerful archangel without specifying the type of archangel. Our audible prayers are heard by agents of both good and evil; this prayer was heard--and acted upon--by a demon. An angel described by a personality as 'fierce looking' immediately appeared and the white blankets began turning red. I quickly realized my mistake and commanded the removal of this demonic archangel. The creature put up a brief fight spewing blood out of its mouth before being subdued and removed by the Holy Spirit. Good worker angels appeared immediately to repair the damage done to the sleeping room. The Holy Spirit told the personality communicating with me that I should be more careful and not make a mistake like that again; a direct reprimand from the Holy Spirit.

This reprimand has been a constant reminder for me. Whether in prayer or in dealing directly with the supernatural, I cannot overemphasize the need for specific and clear communication. The spoken words of any Christian can dramatically affect the surrounding spiritual environment. Accordingly when confronting demons, I have learned that my communication must be clear, specific, and audible; it appears that demons cannot read our thoughts, and so must hear a command before being compelled to obey. Clear and specific commands eliminate any ambiguity that might allow a demon to use their own interpretation of spoken words as an advantage.

4. Spiritual manifestations

The dictionary defines a manifestation as an indication of the existence, reality, or presence of something—in this case, it is the reality of the spiritual world and the beings (angels, demons, etc.) that are so significant in this type of spiritual warfare. Most of these were reported by Grace's personalities, but Grace herself (by virtue of mental overlap with her personalities) has also witnessed many spiritual manifestations. I have also witnessed these things, but only on rare occasions.

The manifestations seen by Grace and her personalities reveal a world that is sharply divided into Godly and satanic realms. Identifying whether a particular manifestation is Godly or demonic has usually been straightforward because of the starkly contrasting effect on Grace and her personalities. I observed that Godly manifestations were always benign towards and respectful of Grace. For example, Holy Spirit angels would typically come along side one of Grace's personalities and wait quietly until directed either by Grace or by the Holy Spirit. Their intent was always helpful and protective, their demeanor gentle, and their actions thoughtful. In stark contrast, demonic manifestations were aggressive and damaging. A demon would usually attempt to dominate Grace--or, more often, to oppress one of her personalities. Demonic intent was always hurtful and violent in the most extreme and blood-thirsty sense. I shudder to think of the conditions for human beings in a hell full of these demonic creatures.

Grace's accounts of the supernatural have been vivid, reminding me of a play-by-play radio broadcast of a baseball game. I have spent many evenings listening to these descriptions--usually from one of Grace's personalities--of spiritual beings and their actions. The information gained from these sessions was of great practical use for me in making important decisions about her healing.

The manifestations we have seen were consistent with the Biblical accounts of the supernatural. The key difference of these manifestations and those recorded in the Bible was that demons usually remained hidden in my wife's subconscious and were therefore not as overt as the dramatic demonic manifestations described in the Bible. It seems, from our experience, that many spiritual manifestations are processed in the subconscious; most of Grace's experiences occurred when her personality states were in executive control of her mind. I remember one of Grace's personalities describing the sparkling specks of light surrounding good angels. Shortly after this description, Grace switched out from her subconscious to her conscious mind to see this manifestation for herself. She could still see the specks of light but they were dimmer and she had to concentrate hard to see them.

4.1 Godly manifestations

Most of the supernatural care and protection for Grace has been accomplished by the Holy Spirit. Grace's personalities often have witnessed the appearance of the Holy Spirit, usually manifested as a man robed in cool bluish or aqua green colors.

Spiritual Healing

His demeanor was characterized by gentleness, thoughtfulness, patience and care giving. These qualities were opposite those characteristics of her earthly father; thus, there was no rejection of the Holy Spirit through association with her father.

Grace's personalities feared change and anything or anybody new. The Holy Spirit's gentle and gradual approach minimized these fears. His identity and nature were apparently unknown in the satanic cults; as a result, there was no defensive cult programming designed specifically for the Holy Spirit. (This contrasts with the very effective programming designed to inhibit any contact with Jesus Christ, programming accomplished by telling children that Jesus was a particularly vicious, murdering, cannibalistic and raping demon. Indeed, there is such a demon that is named Jesus, and the mere mention of the name Jesus often paralyzed Grace's personalities with terror.) Early in the healing process, I learned to depend chiefly on the Holy Spirit for most of Grace's spiritual healing.

While Grace and her personalities have often witnessed the Holy Spirit, appearances of Jesus Christ have been much rarer, occurring only in situations requiring abrupt and forceful action. Christ usually appeared as a Lion or a man. Only once in our experience did He manifest Himself as a Lamb. His colors were golden white and warm tones. When operating in the offensive mode as the Lion, the hair on Christ grew long into a mane and His hands became paws. The holes/scars in His hands remained in His paws. Retractable claws in His paws were used to literally shred demons. His eyes also changed from a warm, inviting color to a brilliant, flashing color of fire. Although fierce in this offensive mode, Christ could also be very gentle. A good example of this was the healing of a girl personality in Grace. This personality kept the memory of a severe beating of Grace. In this case, Holy Spirit angels had brought vials full of the blood of Jesus

Christ and, with Grace's permission, poured the blood onto this personality. Upon contact, this blood turned into cool, cleansing, refreshing water. The personality was so strengthened that she immediately got up, reached out to Christ who had appeared as a man and joyfully began to dance with Him in delight.

I also witnessed Jesus Christ and the Holy Spirit working together on several occasions. (See, for example, the rescue of the boy described at the beginning of this chapter, when the Lion and the Holy Spirit placed the boy between them during the escape from the demonic stronghold.) Grace has also described other situations when Christ and the Holy Spirit were talking together. These observations have broadened my concept of the Trinity. Instead of thinking of God existing separately in any one of three forms, Father, Son and Holy Spirit, I now think of God existing in the three forms simultaneously.

Grace has rarely witnessed a manifestation of God the Father. The key characteristic of these manifestations was brilliance; light of all colors emanating from God the Father. This light was so intense that Grace could not look at His face. Beams of this light coming from His eyes searched the darkness to burn anything impure. These occurrences have not only been infrequent but also brief and incomplete, perhaps due to Grace's fear of her earthly father and a general dislike of any father figure.

Manifestations of good angels became almost a daily occurrence during the core of Grace's healing. These angels appeared in all different types of clothing and could appear as either a man or woman, but always youthful in appearance. Once-- only once--I saw an angel who could have been my guardian angel. The glimpse occurred just as I was waking up from a nap. I looked toward the bedroom door and saw a young man in his twenties with a slender, runner's build with curly, short brown hair slightly thinning in front. He wore blue jeans with woolen plaid shirt. I was terrified, especially since I did not yet have the knowledge of distinguishing good angels from demons. I now know that demons almost always manifest as ugly creatures, very different in appearance from the angel that I saw.

Good angels played a crucial role in Grace's healing. As each new personality awoke, she (or he) was assigned an angel for protection, caring, and comfort. (Their assistance was especially crucial in the care of the baby personalities.) In difficult situations, good angels have even given Grace suggestions by communicating with her through her personalities.

Because the needs of the personalities varied tremendously, the appearance and function of the good angels varied accordingly. For example, exceptionally fearful personalities often were assigned good angels having a powerful, protective appearance or wearing armor and bearing swords. One personality--who had been severely kicked--requested and received a powerful good angel with armor and a brilliant sword while wearing slippers. Those personalities who had experienced sexual abuse from men would receive an angel in the form of a woman. (At least one baby personality had a female good angel with breasts for nursing.) Boy personalities were often assigned good angels wearing hiking/outdoors attire (or, in one case, safari clothes). While good angels did sometimes wear long white or colorful robes, wings and halos were completely absent. From the general descriptions, any of them would have blended well into a crowd of people.

In addition to the good angels assigned to Grace's personalities for general caring and protection, there were many good angels helping Grace with more specific tasks. For example, some of Grace's personalities were in charge of certain body organs or systems. Because her reproductive system had been so abused, the organs in this part of her body underwent much healing. First, there was a careful removal of demons from these organs. Once this was accomplished, hosts of good worker angels came in to these organs repairing damage. These included good angels having needles to "sow" together the torn tissue. We are still uncertain how much of this represented supernatural physical healing and how much was symbolic of spiritual and psychological healing from the sexual abuse.

Grace's personalities have reported other fascinating examples of angelic activity. During a worship service, one personality reported seeing good angels worshiping by dancing in slow, graceful gyrations as they moved in three dimensions. During a prayer session she reported seeing above each person a beam of light directed to God the Father. For some people the beam appeared obstructed and needed attending by good angels who could aid the movement of prayers and answers.

4.2 Demonic manifestations

The bible describes a war in heaven in which Satan was thrown out of heaven along with his angels.[12] These fallen angels--demons--are bent on destroying the people of God. During Grace's healing process, I have seen hundreds of demons exposed and exorcised from her. In each episode Grace (or usually one of her personalities) would describe the appearance and behavior of the demon or demons.

In these encounters and with few exceptions demons manifested themselves as grotesque, blood thirsty, demented creatures. (For a good preview of demonic manifestation imagine a Halloween party with vivid and grotesque costumes.) The demons reported by Grace and her personalities had a mad and obsessive appetite for human flesh and blood. I remember the first words from Grace after an attempted and brief demonic possession of

---
[12] Revelation 12:7-9

Spiritual Healing

her conscious mind that caused her to paw and snort like a bull: "They are like wild, sick animals!"

Based upon these experiences, I have developed strategies for dealing with demons and their influences. I found that, once revealed, demons were much easier to deal with than the lingering psychological damage. So in many ways the exorcisms were exhausting but straightforward. Grace's psychological healing would have been greatly impaired and complete healing probably impossible without first fighting the spiritual battle.

Most people, including believers, have no direct experience of this sort and do not see demons in the same way Grace did. I believe this is a good thing; while I know that I would do anything in order to avoid spending eternity with such creatures, God desires our willing acceptance of his sacrifice and his spiritual protection. We love because he first loved us, and perfect love drives out fear. Fear—even fear of hell—cannot therefore be the primary motivation for coming to God.

The invisibility of spiritual beings is a kind of spiritual barrier that protects us from the demonic. Demons can certainly influence us, especially our emotions, but they cannot simply "march in" and occupy us without our permission. Even growing up in a Satanic household, demonic indwelling was not automatic; there were specific satanic ceremonies to accomplish this. I suspect these were needed to overcome God's natural barriers against demonic indwelling.

Like cockroaches that hide during the daytime and come out only when it is dark, demons seem to excel in hiding. When exposed to the light of God, demons will flee for cover; they are vulnerable to destruction if exposed to God's light radiating through his people and, therefore, prefer hiding. The many personalities within Grace provided an ideal, secret domain for demons. As a result, whenever new personalities within Grace emerged; I had to be on the alert for clues indicating the presence of one or more demons. It was Grace's personalities who had the spiritual vision necessary to see demons and report their presence to me. Without this it would have been very difficult to discern their presence and deliver Grace from their influence.

In contrast to her encounters with the Holy Spirit and Jesus Christ, Grace and her personalities rarely reported seeing Satan. When Grace's personalities see Satan, they describe him either as a manlike being who was extremely desirable and beautiful or as a creature too ugly to look at. Satan's attractive appearance was superficial, covering up a hideous ugliness inside. One of Grace's personalities likened Satan to a "chocolate cake filled with maggots." When in his ugly manifestation, Satan appeared as a huge face covered with blood and with a gapping mouth containing rows of teeth for devouring victims. Also, in this manifestation there were horns protruding out of his skull. But these encounters were not common; unlike God, Satan is a created being and is limited to one location at one time. I suspect that he had more important battles to fight. Our spiritual struggles were mostly with Satan's demonic followers.

Violence and destruction were the chief marks of the demons we encountered. This obsession was so strong that it appeared to impair their reasoning ability. This has been a tremendous advantage for us; many demons apparently did not learn from their mistakes and continually placed themselves in situations that were harmful to their existence. For example, I learned early in Grace's healing process to guide new personalities to the safe place house. (This is described in more detail in the following chapter). To settle them in, I might ask the Holy Spirit to give the new personality a gift such as a stuffed animal, a dress, an ice cream cone, a cookie etc. (These items were given and received on a spiritual/psychological level.) Once received, any demons

Spiritual Healing

present would attempt to spoil the gift—for example, by spilling blood on it—and thus reveal their presence. I could now target the demon for removal and command that it be removed. To my astonishment, this pattern repeated itself consistently during this stage of Grace's healing; the demons never learned to avoid exposing themselves, and hundreds of demons were removed.

Demons described by Grace and/or her personalities were obsessed with blood. As a result, their manifestations frequently involved blood in one form or another. For example, many demons have manifested themselves as creatures with fanged teeth dripping with blood. There was some indication that either Satan, or one of his top archangels manifests as a vampire.

Demons usually appeared grotesque; in the rare occasions when a demon has not, it has always exhibited some suspicious behavior or appearance. For example, one demon appeared as a beautiful, young angel dressed in a glittering evening dress, an ostentatious style that was not consistent with good angels. In another instance, an angel appeared dressed in clothing containing red stripes. (For the ritually abused person, the color red is a reminder of bloody horror--a good angel would never wear this memory triggering color.) Good angels were always youthful in appearance, so the appearance of an elderly, dignified looking angel to one of Grace's personalities was again a clue for demonic presence. Any suspicion regarding the identity of an angel can always be tested. Often I have asked the Holy Spirit to touch the angel in question. If demonic, the angel turns ugly or disintegrates when touched by the Holy Spirit.

The grotesque appearances have been extremely diverse. Grace and her personalities have described demons looking like ugly old ladies, creatures consisting of mostly mouth with big teeth and jaws, monsters with blood dripping from their mouths, or bat-like creatures and vampires. Often these creatures possess claws or other sharp appendages and appear red or black. One demon I saw looked similar to the tin can woodcutter in the Wizard of Oz. (This creature spoke to me in my sleep; telling me that Christ was really just a man and no more.) Frequently, a demon's appearance was magnified and exaggerated. Grace's personalities have described terrifying creatures of tremendous size that shrink to comical little figures when touched by the Holy Spirit.

Besides Satan, the most powerful principality encountered by Grace was Shiva, a Hindu goddess. This demon poses as a seductress who seduces, lures, and deceives humans into a sensual lifestyle. When asked how Shiva would respond to a confrontation with Christ, one of Grace's personalities replied that she would try seducing Him. (This strategy was in sharp contrast to the coarse, fearful, and brutal tactics practiced by most of Satan's hordes.)

In the seventeenth chapter of Revelation, a harlot representing evil holds a goblet of blood in her hand.[13] This imagery is revealing and is not entirely symbolic; in many ways, the goddess Shiva is reminiscent of the harlot. Her activities include temple prostitution and infant sacrifice, a depravity also associated with goddess worship in ancient Greece and Rome. These activities continue today in homes or plush country clubs instead of temples.

The demons exposed in Grace were often grouped into strongholds. Most of these strongholds were in her subconscious, but often had physical influences associated with particular organs and systems. For example, Grace had an eating disorder; if a meal was delayed for more than thirty minutes, she would become irritable, disoriented and even faint. These symptoms disappeared immediately upon the removal of a demonic stronghold that seemed associated with Grace's heart. (We concluded that these demons were somehow constricting Grace's heart, preventing the proper flow of blood throughout her body.)

---

[13] Revelation 17:1-6

Spiritual Healing

Satanic cults have techniques combining sexual pleasure and pain that associate demon possession with sexual and reproductive function. It took us over a year to identify and eradicate these strongholds from Grace. One stronghold—linked to sexual pleasure--was so infested with demons that personalities would sense demons clinging to the organ by hooks in order for all to fit. The chief demon of Grace's womb was reported to have the responsibility of allowing impregnation only for Satan's purposes.

Not all demons appeared in bodily form. Evil spirits could manifest to Grace as a dark fog or as an invisible presence. One was a spirit of death that appeared to have entered Grace during certain death ceremonies. This spirit was especially difficult to exorcise; it was intertwined with the normal and healthy feelings of shock and horror that a child experiences when faced with the reality of death. In this case, the exorcism required the special guidance of a therapist to sort out the healthy feeling of death from the actual evil spirit of death. This was accomplished with my prayers, the prayers of the therapist and those of the personality inhabited by the evil spirit.

A demon named Jesus has been a particular trouble to Grace; it would appear to her in church services just enough to make worship unpleasant for both of us. These manifestations seemed to be enabled by prayers or statements where the name Jesus, instead of Jesus Christ, was spoken. One Sunday morning, the service Grace and I were attending was closed with a prayer in the name of Jesus. Immediately, Grace became extremely agitated; on the verge of running out the building. Suddenly a sense of calm came over her as, I learned later, a voice inside Grace commanded Jesus to leave. I still do not know the origin of this voice, but I am relieved that pastors can no longer inadvertently call out this demon in Grace. It should be noted that in the New Testament letters to the churches rarely is Christ the Messiah called Jesus.

Instead, the Messiah who died and rose again out of the tomb is typically named as Christ or Jesus Christ, rarely just as Jesus. Jesus is a common name in other cultures and addressing Christ simply as Jesus, in my opinion, does not acknowledge His position as the risen King and true Messiah.

During the hundreds of encounters with demons, there have been only a few instances of intelligent communication with them. In one case, a demon bargained with me, a dialogue prompted by the arrival--into the spiritual realm of Grace's mind--of a vial filled with the blood of Jesus Christ. (This blood became cleansing/healing water when poured over the personalities of Grace.) Seeing the vial, this demon became terrified and pleaded with me (through the voice of the personality) to go into a Holy Spirit bag rather than get any of Christ's blood on it. The blood of Christ that is essential healing to Grace's personalities, apparently burns demons.

In another instance, a demon emerged and spoke directly to me. The creature commanded me to grovel on the floor before it and then threatened to cut me into pieces. In response, I laughed thinking it was a personality speaking to me. Later that personality acknowledged that she was hiding and was not talking to me. In a more severe case, a demon intertwined with a personality threatened to cut me up. Because I could not easily distinguish between the personality and the demon and the personality did not immediately accept my authority, my usual commands in the name of Jesus Christ had no effect. However, the personality did respect Grace's authority; she was able to constrain and eventually bind the demon.

These examples illustrate the complexity of extreme spiritual healing. Experiences like these allowed me to establish a deliverance methodology in order to systematically enable Grace's spiritual healing without incurring irreparable psychological and physical damage.

5. Deliverance Methodology

Grace's healing has required spiritual intervention that was both defensive and offensive. The best and primary spiritual defense for Grace was to maintain a spiritual covering through consistent prayer; as her husband I am her first line of defense and have provided most of this spiritual covering. In this, I have had great assistance from small groups, pastors, and friends. Direct intervention—the offensive part—usually involved the deliverance and exorcism of the demonic from Grace. With few exceptions, demons show themselves only in my presence and usually at home, leaving me with the primary responsibility to act. Since I usually needed to act immediately (and often at night), I could not seek help from a pastor or counselor. However, as the healing progressed, both Grace and her personalities became more willing and able to engage in spiritual intervention. Other offensive intervention was also required from time to time (for example, when breaking the bondage of family and generational curses) for which small prayer groups were ideally suited.

5.1 Defensive Activities: Mainly Prayer

My prayer covering for Grace included both general prayers and some very specific ones. Each morning and evening I asked the Holy Spirit for general protection for Grace and her personalities, and also for me. I prayed that His shield of protection would surround each of us for the entire day. My heightened knowledge of the invisible spiritual realm in which we are immersed made this extremely important to me. I also affirmed my authority as head of the family by verbally placing my protection over Grace and her personalities. These measures continue to this day.

My protective prayers became more specific depending on needs and circumstances. For example, visiting Grace's family required specific prayer for protection: a shield of Holy Spirit warrior angels to be placed around Grace and myself for the entire time of contact with her family. I also prayed that only the 'good' personalities within Grace's family members be 'forward' during our visit. Finally, after the visit I asked the Holy Spirit to remove any demons that may have attached themselves to my family. As evidence of the effectiveness of such prayers, I have seen sparkles of light surrounding us when approaching the front door of Grace's parent's home. (These sparkles looked just like fireflies, only during broad daylight.) I interpreted these as God's protective shield clashing with demonic forces; I have never seen these lights in any other circumstances.

There were other protective prayers as well: it was important to ask the Holy Spirit to seal the healing work done for new personalities as they emerged. I also prayed (and often fasted) during satanic festivals: Halloween, the spring equinox and winter solstice, and the end of April Spring rituals. I prayed both for Grace's protection during these times of difficulties and for the protection of infants and children being subjected to abusive satanic rituals.

Just as I provide spiritual covering for my family, a pastor or priest provides spiritual covering for the families in his or her congregation. This covering is very important and is a key benefit of belonging to and attending a church. If pastoral covering is unavailable, I think that God will still provide protection. For example, during the initial stages of Grace's healing, we had just moved and were not able to immediately find a suitable church. With no pastor available, a friend — Lisa — stepped into this role. Over many years, we have found God to be faithful in providing the necessary support personnel at just the right time.

Those who supported us sometimes endured special hardship. Lisa was subject to frightening demonic manifestations, head lice and a miscarriage. Later — after we had found the right church — Pastor Steve provided our spiritual covering. This good and faithful pastor was subject to financial poverty so severe that his family was forced to move into and live in a small travel trailer for a year. Intercessory prayer attracts the enemy's attention and attacks.

Small group settings have also been instrumental for spiritual intervention. I have often been amazed to hear tremendous insights emerge during prayer for Grace. The group setting encourages confirmation of thoughts and insights, something that is especially important when dealing with the unseen or unfamiliar spiritual conditions present in a ritually abused person such as Grace.

Grace has found tremendous spiritual healing during prayer group sessions. This includes a mass exorcism of demons during a woman's retreat, the breaking of generational curses in a support group meeting and the spiritual cleansing for many personalities in prayer sessions following church services.

5.2 Protection and Deliverance

The removal of the demonic--the offensive portion—was the most important aspect of Grace's spiritual healing. Each personality in the early stages of healing typically had one or more demons attached to her/him; their strongholds had to be demolished and the demons removed. This deliverance work was done in parallel with Grace's psychological healing since, without the spiritual healing, a therapist could be misled by demonic influences. But without adequate psychological healing, emotional wounds keep spiritual doors open for demonic influence.

As each of Grace's personalities emerged from Grace's subconscious mind for healing, direct spiritual intervention could usually break the demonic strongholds in which the personalities were imprisoned. The spiritual methodology developed for this can be broken down into three phases; the insertion of good angels, the actual deliverance and establishing good spiritual connection with God. These phases were constantly modified and varied to fit the needs of each emerging personality. For example, during Grace's initial healing stage the need for deliverance dominated. Demons would suddenly manifest, triggering immediate removal. By the later stages of Grace's healing process, most demonic strongholds had been broken. This allowed me to progress at a more leisurely pace through the three phases.

5.2.1 Inserting good angels

I would usually begin the offensive spiritual healing by asking the Holy Spirit to assign one of His angels to a personality who had just emerged. To avoid the risk of having a demon slip in and attaching to the personality, the prayer had to be a very specific request for a good angel from God (a Holy Spirit angel). To further insure against demonic intrusion, I would also ask the Holy Spirit to enable the new personality to see his or her Holy Spirit angel. Not only did this give me further information about who had been sent; it also reassured the new personality that the angel looked safe. The personalities had experienced the reality of the demonic, and were usually terrified until I could reassure them that Holy Spirit angels were benign. I would often describe the good characteristics of Holy Spirit angels to Grace's personalities before asking that they be assigned one in order to ease their acceptance.

For reasons I do not fully understand, sometimes a new personality would not able to see their Holy Spirit angel. Even in these cases, however, the new personality was usually able to feel the presence of the good angel and was then able to see and think more clearly. To Grace and her personalities, goodness was

Spiritual Healing

not just an idea, it was a presence, one that had an immediate and positive impact on her clarity of thinking.

I have found two characteristics of this spiritual phase to be particularly striking. First, I was amazed at God's willingness to accommodate the wishes of each personality. He really does care for us on an individual level and does not hesitate to grant our (sometimes silly but important-to-us) wishes. Second, each personality confirmed the vivid reality of spiritual beings; their perception of the spiritual realm was as real to them as was my perception of the house I lived in.

5.2.2 Deliverance

Deliverance required the binding and removal of demons from Grace and her personalities, a process that was often unpleasant (and sometimes downright spooky). While exorcism has been the most spectacular aspect of Grace's overall healing process, it was not the most difficult. In fact, it was usually quite straightforward--the psychotherapy necessary to help Grace heal from the damage demons left behind was far more challenging.

The following example illustrates one of the more dramatic physical manifestations and the simple deliverance methodology I developed. A new personality had just emerged within Grace and was looking at me with a frightened, puzzled expression. Immediately, I began assuring her that she was safe and asked her if she would like a Holy Spirit angel. I also suggested that I pray against any "things" (demons or evil spirits) attached to her. She immediately became agitated, saying something inside her was getting angry.

Within seconds, the demon erupted to a full physical manifestation. Grace's eyes narrowed, her face distorted and her fingers curled as if forming a claw. A low snarling sound emerged from her mouth. With a quiet, steady voice I commanded, in the name of Jesus Christ, that all demons attached to this personality be immediately bound, silent and then to go into Holy Spirit bags. Grace's countenance changed immediately—the distorted features replaced by a calm and serene appearance. I then asked the Holy Spirit to make sure these commands have been obeyed and to tie closed the bags containing demons only. I did not request the removal of the bags. (At some later time the bags would be checked by the Holy Spirit for items belonging to Grace.) The new personality was then given a Holy Spirit angel friend, good spiritual connections to God and taken to the safe place house inside Grace's mind.

This was the basic spiritual intervention methodology I have used successfully hundreds of times for Grace. There have been many variations of this procedure, but only once has it failed (this will be discussed later).

Despite the straightforward approach, deliverance still needed to be done carefully. For example, before any exorcism I would carefully probe for the intertwining of demons with any of Grace's personalities. Intertwining occurred when a personality identified with a demon. This made it difficult to remove or affect a demon without removing or affecting the personality. If I found any such intertwining, demons were first carefully separated and detached from each personality, then removed. (I found that the hardest part of this process was mustering the patience and sensitivity to separate demons from personalities.) Without the demonic / personality separation, an abrupt exorcism had the potential of harming Grace. Therefore, deliverance first required an understanding of the spiritual state of each new personality; to do this, I had to be able to recognize clearly when a demon was present.

Recognition

Deliverance was usually required whenever a demon manifested. These varied in severity, from full-blown physical manifestations to less obvious appearances that required patience and careful listening. Physical manifestations were those that found their way from Grace's mind to her body: a distortion of her face; the shaping of her hands into claws; strange noises and voices; and possibly other bizarre behavior. The clawing of her hands was by far the most common manifestation. When I suspected that a demon might be surfacing (as when a new personality was emerging) I would often watch her hands for clawing.

In the more subtle cases there were often no external signs of the demonic; rather, Grace's personalities would report seeing demons or reveal signs of demonic influence. Some of the more subtle demonic signs were an express desire to hurt me or simply a sudden and abnormal fear.

"Full-blown" manifestations

Physical demonic manifestations that I refer to as "full-blown" were obvious and dramatic, occurring more frequently during the early stages of Grace's healing. In fact, the worst such demonic manifestation triggered one of my very first exorcisms. I remember Grace suddenly pawing like a bull while struggling to say "get it off me" between snorting sounds coming out of her mouth. This manifestation lasted about five seconds, about the time it took me to say "in the name of Jesus Christ I command the demon causing this to be bound and silent." This scenario was repeated a second time when "helper" demons appeared and were also told to be bound and silent. Badly shaken, Grace could only describe the demons as being like wild, sick animals. In this case, the demons were attempting full possession of Grace's conscious mind.

Such severe demonic manifestations have been quite easy to recognize. They typically started with Grace's eyes opening wide and eyebrows arched high. Her fingers would curl into a claw-like shape and her mouth would open wide with her tongue protruding, flickering up and down. This motion caused emitted moans to pulsate in intensity. I have heard a variety of sounds emanating from Grace during a full blown demonic manifestation. These include hissing noises, low moans (kind of like a tape recorder being played back on slow speed) and snorting bull sounds. As seconds pass by, such manifestation usually became more pronounced. Sometimes the manifestations would cause Grace's body to rock back and forth or her back to arch backwards. Sometimes her eyes would narrow giving her face a sinister appearance or her eyes would roll back in the eye sockets so much that only the whites of her eyes were visible.

Subtle manifestations

Most demonic manifestations in Grace were quite subtle and usually internal--seen only by her personalities. Recognizing these demons required open and sensitive communication with each personality, especially those who had just emerged. As important as my communication was, the words and thoughts exchanged between Grace and her personalities were even more important. The deliverance process became much easier when Grace, as the host personality, learned to communicate directly with her inner personalities. This enabled her to do much of the spiritual work—after all, she could see and sense the state and spiritual condition of her personalities much better than I.

The subtle signs were all important to identify and target demons for binding and removal. For example, a personality might report seeing blood spattered on a gift she had received; this was all the information I needed to exorcise the demon that had despoiled the gift. The indirect sign of spattered blood provided the means to identify and target any demons attached to this personality.

Fear was a very common, but subtle, indication of a demon's presence. However, I found it very difficult to distinguish between healthy fear and demonically inspired fear. When a personality awakes to totally new surroundings, or sees something that triggers the memory of terrifying abuse, fear is a natural reaction. However, fear so excessive that a personality becomes paralyzed with fear and cannot reason is a good indication that a demon is present. Uncontrollable shaking can also be an outward sign of excessive fear.

When I observed excessive fear in a new personality, I went on the alert for more specific signs and would listen carefully for additional clues. If a personality was seeing blood, knives, or other objects of horror, this was usually sufficient to identify and target the demon. After an exorcism of one demon, it was not unusual for manifestations to continue as other demons attempted to disrupt any communication I might have with new personalities.

There were other, less common signs. For new personalities who appeared drugged or sleepy, I had to discern between natural drowsiness and a demon-induced lethargy. Also, demons sometimes oppressed personalities in order to hinder communication. I remember one case where a group of five personalities described being spiritually entwined with a serpent-like demon. This bondage was so strong that it took over an hour of patient conversation before I could accurately assess the situation. In these cases, I found it best to pray for the breaking of the demonic bondage causing the symptoms, whatever they might be. If the symptoms were natural, nothing would happen. If they were caused by demonic activity, the symptoms would either disappear or diminish.

The obvious physical manifestations were most common early in Grace's healing, when there were demonic strongholds still resident. As the healing progressed, these manifestations eased in their severity and frequency; the demonic strongholds were crumbling one by one. Today there are few (if any) signs of the demonic and any deliverance work is largely precautionary.

Targeting

Managing an exorcism in which a demon was intertwined with one of Grace's personalities required clear and careful targeting of the demonic. Such targeting was crucial to avoid damaging Grace; the careless removal of a demon could remove a part of her. In extreme (and rare) situations, a personality could be so intertwined with a demon so as to appear to be a demon. While the Holy Spirit would never remove an essential part of Grace, a personality under my authority could still obey a deliverance command and withdraw into an inaccessible portion of Grace's mind.

I have learned to wait patiently for clear demonic manifestations before targeting. It has helped that their appearance is fairly predictable; most manifestations occurring soon after a new personality emerged. The manifestations were usually distinct enough to quickly enable the targeting of the demon. Once targeted, I removed them as quickly as possible. (I never saw the need to communicate with the demon or to ask its name. Demons are ugly, filthy creatures and I deposed them as quickly as possible.)

I have found it important to carefully listen to Grace and observe her closely; in this way, I have often been able to avoid "full blown" manifestations by acting quickly to exorcise demons. Watching Grace carefully meant, in part, keeping my eyes open during prayer. When there was any hint of the demonic I never closed my eyes during prayer and concentrated my senses on Grace. Visual clues such as Grace's hands clawing, fingers forming into a claw like shape, were very valuable in stopping a "full blown" manifestation. In fact, often I just watched her hands; especially if a new personality was emerging. I found that the easiest and, often, first sign of a demonic eruption started with the "clawing" of her hands.

Spiritual Healing

Deliverance words

The exact deliverance wording I used was brief, simple and specific: In the name of the Lord Jesus Christ, I command the demons causing this manifestation [whatever it was] to be immediately bound and silent and to go into Holy Spirit bags. (During full-blown physical manifestations I learned to say this sentence very quickly, so the command needed to be brief and simple.) The manifestation nearly always ceased as soon as I spoke these words. The authority of Jesus Christ is absolute and overwhelming for demons.

Deliverance commands were specific in several ways. First, these commands were always given in the name of Jesus Christ, never in the name of Jesus. Jesus is a common name in some cultures and I do not think that demons are obligated to obey somebody named Jesus. I do not believe that praying "in the name of Jesus" is any more effective than praying "in the name of Orville" when it comes to spiritual warfare. Spiritual authority is derived from the death and resurrection that only the Christ the Messiah accomplished. The power of Christ is accessed through His full name for He is the Messiah. I am convinced that spiritual beings must submit to this authority.

There was (and probably still is) a powerful and vile demon named Jesus who was very fond of hurting children; the mere mention of his name struck terror in many of Grace's personalities. I quickly found that if I used only the name Jesus in my prayers, I ran the risk of causing more psychological problems for Grace and her personalities. Praying in the name of Jesus could open doors for demonic activity without realizing it.

Could a prayer in the name of Jesus actually cause damage for ordinary Christians? I am not certain, since spiritual warfare can be so different from person to person. But my experience with Grace has been dramatic and clear enough that I always shudder when I hear Christians praying in the name Jesus instead of Jesus Christ.

When praying, God can clearly read our minds and know our intent before we even speak any words. I believe that God answers our prayers based on our intent and what is best for us. However, a demon cannot determine my intent except through my spoken words. If my words contain ambiguous commands, a demon can treat it like a legal loophole. I remember commanding one demon to go into a bag for containment and later removal, but I did not specify what kind of bag was to be used for this. The personality described the immediate appearance of a bag held by a black appendage. In this case, one of Grace's other personalities alerted me to a problem. I clarified my instruction and the demon was placed in a Holy Spirit bag.

Verbal specificity was especially crucial if there were strong attachments between a personality within Grace and any demon or demons associated with that personality. In these situations, I found it essential to make it clear that only demons were to be bound, silent and placed into Holy Spirit bags for confinement. (I placed a great deal of emphasis on the word only as I spoke the deliverance words.) This wording was usually successful at preventing a personality from succumbing to the bound and silent command. To make sure, I always asked the Holy Spirit to check and make sure that only demons had been bound and silenced and that the Holy Spirit bags contained demons only.

I found it important to define demons as beings that were not part of Grace's body or mind. This was done so that her personalities did not obey commands intended for demons. I did this especially if a new personality was a toddler or younger child. A small child is more easily confused and is more likely to go into a Holy Spirit bag.

It was sometimes possible to identify demons by interrogating them about time spent outside Grace's mind and body. Clearly if the entity being interrogated was at some time separate from Grace then that entity was demonic. This better defined the separation between personalities and demons. Being sufficiently specific in a crisis situation was difficult. As Grace's healing has progressed, some of her personalities now check my wording, alerting me to problems if my spoken words are vague.

I always spoke the deliverance words as calmly and softly as possible. Of course, in the midst of a "full blown" demonic manifestation it was hard to be calm. But I never shouted the deliverance words. There was no need to shout. Demons have good hearing and could probably hear what I was saying even if I was whispering. On the other hand, new personalities could have easily become alarmed if I was shouting and there was no need to give demons more ammunition by inciting fear in a new personality.

When demons are bound and silenced, their evil and obstructing influence is stopped immediately. At a later time, Grace would ask the Holy Spirit to check the bagged demons for anything that belonged to her and her personalities. Occasionally bagged demons still possessed items that belonged to Grace. To prematurely expel these demons would risk permanent damage; the bagging process effectively restrained demonic influence until demons were thoroughly checked for anything that belonged to Grace.

An example of this occurred while cleansing Grace from demons that attacked her sexual and reproductive functions. Dozens of demons had been "bagged," and I was in the process of asking the Holy Spirit to expel all of these demons when a personality cautioned me to wait. The personality then asked me to have the Holy Spirit check the bagged demons for items belonging to Grace. Sure enough, a demon grasping a string of some sort was found. The string was cleansed, purified and placed into a harp that was missing this string. The harp could now be played making beautiful music. After this action the demon was expelled, freeing Grace's body from that particular attack. It seems that the demon possessed some aspect of Grace's sexuality that was represented symbolically by the harp-string. If I had acted hastily in expelling this demon, the loss of the string could have resulted in permanent damage.

As Grace's healing progressed, the manifestations diminished. I was no longer able to target demons based on their manifestations, but I knew that each new personality emerging could have demons attached to him or her. Fortunately, these new personalities generally were easily helped and I did not worry nearly as much about personalities being intertwined with demons or thinking they were demons. More as a preventative measure, I simply commanded demons attached to a newly emerged personality to be removed. Accordingly, I modified my deliverance wording slightly. When a new personality emerged, the basic wording was changed to "in the name of the Lord Jesus Christ I command all demons or evil spirits attached in any way to this (new) personality be immediately bound and silent and go into Holy Spirit bags." Then I also added the sentence "Holy Spirit please make sure this command has been obeyed and then close up and tie up the Holy Spirit bags containing demons and/or evil spirits only." Compensating for the lack of targeting information due to the absence of demonic manifestations, I asked the Holy Spirit to be more involved in my deliverance commands.

I was also careful to specify that demons targeted for removal be only those attached to the newly emerged personality. Usually I would work with one new personality at a time, requesting that other new personalities wait their turn.

Connection to God

While new personalities were acquainted with (and terrified of) demonic influences, most had not yet been introduced to the

Savior at the time they emerged. Deliverance leaves a spiritual void that can only be filled with a relationship with God. The final step in deliverance was then to ask the Holy Spirit to give each new personality a spiritual connection to the Triune God. My words for this were "Holy Spirit please give this (new) personality a good spiritual connection only to you Holy Spirit, to the Heavenly Father, Lord Jesus Christ, Lion of Judah, Jehovah Yahweh, Good, Great and Mighty God." I am not sure why I chose this combination of names for God; often new personalities would not accept this connection until I explained that the titles were just names for the good Sunday God. This was reassuring for the personalities since most of them had learned about God in Sunday school. Grace's mother, likely in her "daytime" personality state, made sure that all her children were exposed to Christianity by bringing them to church on Sundays.

When talking with Grace's personalities--especially the new ones--I would sometimes describe the attributes of the Triune God. During this teaching time, I quickly learned to be cautious when mentioning the name Jesus Christ. Satanic cults know Jesus Christ as their great adversary, and many of Grace's personalities had been trained to react negatively to the mere mention of His name. For example, an adolescent personality once slapped my face after I mentioned the name of Jesus Christ; for her, I began simply referring to Christ as the Lion of Judah. However, during the deliverance work I always used the name Jesus Christ.

In addition to spiritual connection, I sometimes requested that the Holy Spirit give special spiritual gifts. In one case, a personality received decorated boxes from the Holy Spirit. Upon opening the boxes, this personality received gifts of confidence, joy, self-esteem, etc. These gifts satisfied basic needs for this personality and, by extension, for Grace.

Introducing new personalities to God concluded the basic spiritual healing necessary when new personalities emerged. The remaining healing concentrated on psychotherapy with ongoing spiritual healing sprinkled throughout.

Anomalies

The deliverance I have described was repeated, with some variations, many hundreds of times. I did encounter unusual cases that merit special mention because they did not fit the usual pattern. One of those cases involved direct communication with demons. While I never pursued communication with demons (this only gave them time to think and deceive), there have been three or four instances when I have conversed directly with them. For example, one demon passed messages to me through a personality of Grace. The personality had seen a Holy Spirit angel bring a vial containing the blood of Jesus Christ—blood that when poured out on her could provide healing. The demon attached to this personality was deathly afraid of the blood and tried to bargain with me to prevent this. In another case, a demon threatened me with dismemberment and commanded me to grovel on the floor before it. In both these cases, the demons shortly ended up confined in Holy Spirit bags.

There has been at least one case in which a personality of Grace was so entwined with a demon that even Grace could not initially distinguish the demon from this personality. (This occurred during the usual bagging of a demon.) As the usual spiritual deliverance process began, both Grace and I felt that something was wrong. Instead of proceeding as usual, the Holy Spirit was asked to place this personality in a special enclosed, holding area in Grace's mind. Days later Grace was able to separate out the personality from the demon and then the demon was removed.

This illustrates the cautious approach required in deliverance; unless a manifestation was putting Grace in immediate danger, I would usually opt for containment. It has been my experience that demonic influence can be contained temporarily without the removal of demons.

Baby personalities presented unique and difficult challenges. In both body and mind, there is a wide disparity between adults and young children, so the emergence of a very young personality could be exhausting and dangerous for Grace. A baby personality also had difficulty in communication. Sometimes--especially later in the healing process--other personalities provided invaluable help as interpreters for a baby personality. I especially relied on the Holy Spirit to protect the babies and do the spiritual work that needed to be done. Even—especially--when my wisdom, strength and resources were exhausted, the Holy Spirit was always available.

There were rare occasions when demons simply did not respond to my commands. In these situations, it fell on Grace as the host personality to assert her authority to bind and silence the demonic. These anomalies are puzzling when compared to the many demons that responded immediately to my authority. In one situation, the demon who ignored my authority was closely intertwined with a personality (who had authority over that demon) and refused to give up the demon. Grace, in turn, had direct authority over this personality, and was able to override her reluctance and intervene directly by exorcising the demon. One possible reason for my difficulty was Grace's prior involvement in goddess cults. Women led these cults; I may have lacked the proper gender credentials as far as some personalities were concerned.

Demons were usually exorcised individually or in small groups. However, in one situation Grace and I uncovered a stronghold of about fifty demons that needed clearing out. After these demons had been bagged, a dump truck appeared in Grace's mind. All the bags were tossed into the truck and carried away.

Demons were sometimes destroyed outright, but only when Grace or I had requested this. Grace once described a demon disintegrating into pieces and vanishing after being 'zapped' by the Holy Spirit. She has also described a small lake, surrounded by hills (perhaps corresponding to the Lake of Fire in Revelation), to which demons captured by Holy Spirit angels are taken. Some demons were not destroyed or bagged but cast into a vault and sealed. If the demon was particularly active, the Holy Spirit sprayed a mist-like substance over the demon that appeared to paralyze it before sealing the vault.

Whether they were destroyed outright, bagged, or vaulted, the key was to free Grace and her personalities from their control. Once removed, I did not really care what happened to the demons.

6. Key Lessons

During the course of Grace's spiritual healing, I have learned many important lessons. I group these lessons into two categories: 1) The realization that Grace and I (and every other human being) are immersed in a spiritual, supernatural world that is vibrant and real; 2) Learning my place in that spiritual realm, especially in understanding the spiritual leadership and authority necessary for her healing.

As a Christian who was raised in evangelical churches, I believed in the supernatural. But I found that there was a gap between an abstract belief that spiritual forces exist and the faith and action necessary to assert that belief in my daily life and actions. As my wife's healing process began, I soon discovered that my beliefs in the supernatural were shallow and abstract; that attitude changed quickly when I was confronted with the demonic manifestations evident in Grace. At that point, I had no choice but to treat the spiritual realm as something up close and personal.

Spiritual Healing

I learned that I was immersed in a spiritual world much more than I had ever realized. That spiritual realm was, and still is, just as real and vibrant as the physical realm that I can see, hear, smell and touch. The spiritual realm is close at hand and is not the faraway place that images of heaven (or hell) typically invoke. Spiritual beings are not just the fantasy figures we imagine from the movies we watch but are real and powerful creatures whose goal is our eternal destruction, if they are demons, or our salvation if they are Godly angels.

I am convinced that the spiritual realm Grace and I experienced is more commonly experienced than most would think. As humans, there is a reason we are mostly blind to the spiritual realm we are embedded in; if ordinary people saw the spiritual realm that I have witnessed, most individuals would be frightened into paralysis. I do not think that this is the decision-making environment God wants for us. Rather, he created us free and wants us to accept His offer of salvation based on love and not from fear.

But demons are also creatures under authority; no believer should ever be paralyzed by fear of the supernatural. As a follower of Jesus Christ, I, and any other Christian, am privileged to exercise God's power and authority. As incredible as it might seem, that is my role in the spiritual realm. I therefore had authority; a demon was obliged to obey any command given "…in the name of the Lord Jesus Christ."

Of course, I needed to manage this authority properly and carefully. Many of the experiences were frightening and mind-bending. And, early on, I made many mistakes; for example, I had some difficulty at first recognizing the difference between demons and Godly angels. Eventually, it became easy to distinguish between the "good guys" and the "bad guys."

I never became completely comfortable in the deliverance process; when a demonic manifestation occurs I still feel the goose bumps rising on my skin. Yet with confidence I became accustomed to controlling and exorcising the demonic within my wife based on the overwhelming power of God. And I am convinced that any Christian has this spiritual power available to them; demons cringe when Christians pray in the name of Jesus Christ, lest something be said that would lead to their immediate destruction. That is why, I believe, demons are so good at hiding. They exist in a weakened spiritual position and they know it.

Understanding and implementing this spiritual power enabled me to guide and direct my wife's spiritual healing. Indeed, this became the easiest part of her healing process. The next chapter describes what became the most difficult and exhausting part of the healing process.

7. Summary

As a Christian, I had always understood that there is a spiritual/supernatural realm. This was an understanding based almost completely on intellect, with little reality in my personal experience. My marriage to Grace shattered this cozy, safe concept. My perception of the supernatural changed from being distant to a near-total immersion in what is now a dynamic and very real spiritual realm. This realm is very bi-polar: It can be good or evil, righteous or hideous, Godly or demonic. It is a realm in which the triune Godhead and His good angels stand against Satan and his demons. It is a realm that can reveal either righteousness and beauty or ugliness and perversion. Fortunately, it is a realm in which the ultimate power resides with the Triune God.

While I saw this realm through Grace's experiences, I believe we are all immersed in it. Our spiritual eyes are often blinded to it, which is probably a good thing! But make no mistake: This spiritual realm affects us for good or evil even when we are unaware of it.

Spiritual Healing

My experiences with the spiritual realm were often unnerving; we found demonic manifestations to be both ugly and threatening. Fortunately, in this realm the power of God is absolute. I learned quickly to apply this power via the simple phrase "in the name of Jesus Christ...." With few exceptions, my spiritual commands to control and exorcise demons were obeyed immediately. In hindsight, I found the spiritual healing to be significantly easier than the psychological and physical healings. I believe this application of God's power in the spiritual realm is a harbinger of God's authority and power that will be given to Christians over all realms in the eternal kingdom of God. What a wonderful future to look forward to for all Christians!

Psychological Healing

*A**new personality—a teenaged girl, whose name I have now forgotten—had just emerged from Grace's subconscious. I promised to take her on a father-daughter date to a pizza shop not far from our home. As I sat across from her and we ate our pizza, she began to talk freely about herself, her hopes, dreams and desires. But mostly she complained about Grace, my wife. I remember hearing complaints about my wife having too many rules to live by. But I mostly remember struggling to suppress my feelings of discomfort and alarm. Here I was, talking to somebody occupying my wife's body and acting as if it were perfectly normal. Was I in some kind of bizarre episode of the Twilight Zone?*

Conversations like this became quite common over the course of Grace's healing. Although I got used to them (in the sense of knowing what to expect), it was always unnerving, almost as troublesome as a full blown demonic manifestation. These personalities were not demons to be dismissed—they were, and are, part of Grace's mind and personality. Her complete healing requires a gradual emergence and re-integration of these personalities. This psychological healing was far more difficult and dangerous than the spiritual healing, and I needed the help of professional and highly trained therapists and physicians.

I have often wondered why God did not heal Grace from the psychological trauma just as He had healed Grace from the spiritual abuse. Specifically, why could I not simply ask God for the removal of the guilt and shame of her memories in the same way that I asked Him for the removal of demons? Why would not

God simply and instantly free Grace from the mind-control of the cults?

The answers to these questions are central to understanding the psychological healing process. Grace's feelings and mind belonged to her and God would not destroy or remove any part of Grace. A gradual, if arduous, healing process was the only way to make her shattered personality whole again. In this process God, especially through the Holy Spirit, guided us and our health professionals through the treacherous mental traps set by the cults and the difficulties of restoring a mind warped by the extreme abuse and satanic programming.

Stories of cult programming and mind control usually evoke images of people in trance-like mental states, unable to function in our fast paced society and doomed for a life in mental institutions. In contrast, Grace and her family had capabilities and led lifestyles that appeared productive and normal. Before the healing process began, Grace was able to hold a job, teach Sunday school and manage a sizable Christian scouting program. Grace's father held a stable job for over thirty years and her mother was active in church and community activities. This cult programmed satanic family was clearly able to function well in society.

Growing up in a Satan-centered home, Grace was subject to mind-boggling physical, psychological and spiritual abuse. The satanic cults programmed Grace, from birth, to act and think in a manner that: 1) preserved the secrecy of the cults, 2) enabled her survival during the cult rituals and activities and 3) enabled her to function in her birth-determined role within the cults. (This abuse and programming was described in detail in the Abuse chapter.)

The programming taught Grace to suppress the intense feelings of pain, guilt and anger. As a result, she was emotionally unstable and ready to explode if triggered by the slightest provocation. Relieving the pressure of the "pent up" festering

Psychological Healing

feelings and the process of righting Grace's thinking and values, deprogramming, constitutes the core of her psychological healing.

1. Signs

With hindsight, there were some initial signs of Grace's psychological issues surfacing even before our marriage. These signs were so slight that only a person trained in psychotherapy might have noticed. She functioned well in her job and church ministries; but as time passed, Grace became more emotionally unstable. Memories of the abuse began emerging from Grace's subconscious. A short time later, she began to break down emotionally, and then checked herself into a hospital. There really was no other reasonable option left; the healing process was thrust upon us and the five worst—but necessary--years of our married life began.

The emerging crisis showed itself first in sudden mood shifts and shame. I remember one instance when I had been tutoring Grace. After an hour of diligent study her involvement simply and abruptly stopped, as though she had suddenly become another person. I was puzzled, stopped tutoring since she had lost attention, but did not pursue the matter. It is now clear that I had been tutoring another person; Grace had gotten tired and had shifted into another personality state. Her emotional mood, interests, and even her intellect had changed. (The mood change was the easiest to recognize.)

Grace also showed signs of shame. (This was very evident in Grace's father; he never was able to look me in the face while talking with me. Instead, he looked down, with an occasional glance at me.) It was at church that more signs of emotional distress were apparent. Often Grace would sit in the church pew with down cast demeanor; the pastor of the church noticed this and asked me if there were issues in Grace's life needing attention. He was the first person to recognize signs of psychological distress in Grace.

We now know that this distress was Grace's shame overflowing from hideous memories of abuse and forced participation in cult activities. Even though the details were, at the time, hidden from Grace's conscious mind, the feelings produced by the horrific events had begun to seep into her conscious mind and demeanor.

Another early sign was the venting of pent-up emotions in a manner and intensity that was out of proportion to the situation. It eventually became so severe that Grace would become distraught or angry, and eventually explode, without any perceptible provocation. It was in the wake of one of these episodes that Grace was hospitalized and found a mental health professional who could shed light on the behavior. (Not surprisingly, this episode occurred a week before a major satanic festival. All of Grace's hospitalizations occurred during major satanic festivals, times when her memories would surface, forcing her to relive the trauma.)

Grace also had nightmares that were linked to memories seeping from Grace's unconscious into her conscious mind. I suspect that this type of memory 'venting' is common for all types of abuse. But Grace's signs of satanic abuse were unique in two ways. First, some of Grace's dreams were spiritually active, in which demons entered into the nightmare and actively participated. Second, there was a dominance of blood in her nightmares, a theme that was so strong that it pervaded the thoughts and feelings latent in Grace's subconscious. Therapy established better pathways for the emotional venting and Grace's nightmares subsided considerably. But before the therapy began, nightmares were a strong harbinger of the needed psychological work.

The signs mentioned so far are indicators, but fall far short of the severity of her mental and emotional trauma. The more obvious signs of ritual abuse began emerging during and after

Grace's first hospitalization. The first unmistakable sign of multiplicity occurred when Grace looked into a mirror and saw somebody else. One of her personalities had momentarily emerged from Grace's subconscious and was frightened to see a much older face; the shock of seeing what appeared to be someone else's face was strong enough that Grace felt it even in her own conscious mind. As the healing progressed, this became a problem; when a new personality emerged I would keep Grace away from any mirrors.

The next sign of multiplicity occurred when therapists in the hospital asked Grace to do an exercise in automatic writing. This involved writing with her non-dominant hand and was seen as a possible way to access suppressed feelings. A participant will usually write about his or her feelings, but Grace's hand started writing messages to her. The first message she read was "you are a monster"; a child personality was communicating with the outside world and with Grace. The child reasoned that, since the only adults she knew abused her, all adults (including Grace) must be monsters.

The first clear sign of hidden ritual information occurred during Grace's art therapy sessions. Cult programming establishes a 'no-talk' rule in children to preserve secrecy. This rule can be circumvented via drawings, since there was not any 'no draw' rule in the cult programming for children. In a single session, Grace's art therapist assessed Grace's cult involvement based on the prevalence of blood and bloody symbols in her pictures.

Psychologists report evidences of personality disorder that include losing track of time, finding unexplained clothing in the closets and, perhaps, losing one's car in a parking lot. These signs were not especially prominent in Grace possibly because she had over a thousand fractured personalities instead of a few dozen dominant personalities (most people with this disorder do not have as many personalities as Grace has had).

Hearing voices inside the head can also be a sign of personality disorder. These were mostly personalities attempting to communicate with Grace (the host personality), but she also recalls hearing demonic voices at times. It was easy to segregate these voices from those of personalities by content; demonic voices demanded self-destructive behavior. For example, toward the end of one hospitalization a voice instructed Grace to go home and, with specific instructions, kill herself. Fortunately, Grace was able to share this with her therapist who then arranged for extended hospitalization.

The final signs of multiplicity occurred when new personalities began emerging in Grace. These personalities had specific names, different voices, younger ages than Grace (usually children) and certainly different thought patterns than Grace. They were unmistakably and shockingly not Grace.

2. Resources

During the years leading up to Grace's first hospitalization, we lived far from Grace's hometown and from any known centers of occult activity. I think that this geographic isolation prevented cult members from reinforcing Grace's programming, thereby giving her the time and freedom to realize the need for healing. Shortly after Grace's first hospitalization--and the intense start of the healing process--we moved to an area located closer to Grace's parents, an area of strong satanic activity.

Why did God move us into such an apparently dangerous situation? The answer is simple. Where evil abounds goodness abounds more. This is an example of a balancing theme I have observed not only in nature but also in the spiritual realm. Where there is evil, there will be goodness that more than balances out the evil. Furthermore, that goodness, if implemented fully, will be stronger and fully capable of extinguishing evil. And that is exactly what we found: The most significant psychological healing occurred while we lived in this location.

The city to which we had moved did not have many strong churches. But we found one church (a Vineyard Church) whose members freely allowed God's power to flow through them. It was the pastor and his wife along with other members of this congregation that provided the crucial spiritual covering for Grace and me during a critical stage of her healing.

When a personality emerged, Grace would need immediate attention; most of the therapy occurred at home. But healing also took place in the car while driving on a freeway, in churches, once on an airplane and in stores. The most intense healing happened in therapist's offices and in hospitals. (Grace was hospitalized multiple times, each hospitalization lasting about three weeks.) Dealing with the emotional upheaval as well as the distress associated with the healing was very exhausting; we were in our twenties and thirties and had the energy necessary to focus on the therapy. Once the core healing was accomplished it took several years for the two of us to recuperate and begin living something approaching a normal life.

We were blessed to have an excellent team of psychiatrists and therapists as experts to provide advice and assist with the most intense part of Grace's healing. The therapists usually took the lead; few therapists are qualified for treating the combination of personality disorder and satanic ritual abuse and, I suspect, few therapists would want to deal with it. Practicing such therapy requires intense training, usually a doctoral degree, and a creative and quick intellect to respond to the intricate needs of a mind twisted by satanic programming. Grace's key therapist was also a Christian. This was a huge benefit since this excellent therapist understood the need for spiritual healing as well. However, I think that an excellent non-Christian therapist would be preferred over a poor Christian therapist for this type of therapy.

While the medical specialists took the lead, Grace had so many personalities emerging (more than one per day for several years) that I was forced to learn how to provide therapy. For example, I remember one dangerous situation when a new, adolescent personality had emerged during an hour-long session with Grace's therapist. As I walked Grace back to our car for the journey home, I noticed a look of concern from the therapist. Normally this therapist would spend the extra time needed for finishing up any needed therapy. But she had an appointment and was not available for continued therapy beyond the scheduled hour with Grace. As Grace and I walked from the therapist's office to our car, I immediately sensed that an alternate personality had come forward. This was confirmed when Grace refused to sit in the front seat of our car but sat rather in the rear seat as far from me as possible. I immediately began talking to this new personality, trying to understand how to help her. It soon became apparent to me that she was planning suicide while I was at work the next day, so I desperately started thinking of ways to stall her plans and give her the time necessary to reconsider.

I needed some way of convincing this personality that she was cared for and important, and began bargaining with her for Grace's life. I told her that I would buy her a new dress of her choosing in turn for a firm agreement not to commit suicide. She was intrigued by this offer and agreed. Of course, it took some time to arrange the shopping trip and pick out the dress; by the end of the process I had secured an extra two days. When I fulfilled my part of the bargain, she knew that she was cared for and decided that life was worth living after all.

I found that purchasing dresses and clothing was extremely helpful for many personalities. The clothing items gave them possessions that helped them establish their identity. The closets in our home are filled with clothes for Grace and her personalities.

The decision usually wasn't hard; a fifty dollar dress was a great bargain for Grace's life.

As we progressed, Grace herself became one of the most useful resources for healing; Grace or her personalities quite often came up with important ideas and suggestions. In fact, it became common practice for Grace's therapist to ask Grace what she thought about a certain issue. Besides getting answers, this technique enabled Grace to increase her confidence, to practice thinking and problem-solving on her own.

I cannot close this section without acknowledging the help of the Holy Spirit. Grace and I depended heavily on Him for guidance and help on a daily basis. His availability both day and night was both crucial and comforting. His gentle nature was perfect for helping Grace's youthful personalities who needed care, comforting and security. His guidance was also crucial for Grace and me, especially when we were baffled by new, confusing, and frightening situations (such as the suicidal personality). My idea of using a dress to bargain for Grace's life surely was inspired by the Holy Spirit. His protective actions enabled Grace's psychological healing to continue without interruption. Surely the enemy must have tried interrupting Grace's healing constantly since she once belonged to Satan. Yet it must be that these attempts were countered by protective actions of the Holy Spirit; either directly or indirectly through guidance given to us and Grace's therapists. I suspect that the Holy Spirit gave us other help of which I was not aware; someday I hope to learn more fully about all He must have done behind the scenes.

3. Deprogramming

The healing of Grace's mind was a two-pronged effort. She needed healing from the emotional trauma held in the memories of her many personalities, but she first needed release from the cult programming. I will concentrate on the deprogramming efforts, a description that will necessarily include most of the details of the treatment for abuse. One reason is that, while there is substantial literature on psychological healing methods for severe abuse and trauma, I found much less information available on deprogramming.

The Abuse chapter described in detail the training and programming methods used by the satanic cults that taught Grace how to: 1) preserve the secrecy of the cults; 2) survive the cult rituals and activities; and 3) function in her birth determined role within the cults. As a result, Grace's mind was programmed to think primarily in ways that accomplished these three goals; the original, healthy and God-given patterns of thought were erased and replaced by unhealthy, cult-inspired thinking.

Consider as an example the avoidance of pain and search for pleasure: In its ordinary form it is a strong and healthy instinct, but the cult programming distorted those into destructive acts that mingled pain and pleasure. A key goal of the psychological healing was to break the bondage of the satanic programming and restoring healthy thinking patterns and instincts. This was possible, in part, because the evil programming was never complete; Grace always had a residue of her God-given instincts that could never be completely overwhelmed.

The cult programming fragmented Grace's mind and caused her multiple personality disorder (MPD), a condition that has become familiar to many therapists and medical professionals. Much of the deprogramming was centered on healing from this personality disorder; this required restoring Grace's mind by first exposing and then integrating her personalities back into her conscious mind. There is a very good book written by James

Friesen called Uncovering the Mystery of MPD[14] that describes this disorder and its spiritual origins.

3.1 Stages of healing

The integration of Grace's personalities back into her conscious mind required that we first expose the personalities, allow stored memories to be shared and feelings expressed and, eventually, fuse these personalities back into Grace's conscious mind. The methodology changed over the course of Grace's healing; there were three distinct stages of the healing, and I will describe each in some detail.

The initial stage grew from the realization that hidden feelings and information in Grace's mind existed and needed to be dealt with; simply artificially suppressing them would not accomplish the healing. It was at this stage that we first discovered the personality multiplicity; it was the most unpredictable and dangerous period for Grace, since the potential for suicide and other psychosis-related physical and mental harm were a constant danger.

Most of the real healing was accomplished in the intermediate stage. By this time Grace's personalities (along with their associated memories and feelings) were steadily emerging in a (mostly) controlled fashion and Grace was under the supervision of a well trained psychotherapist. It was during this stage that the satanic programming was broken and the control of Grace's mind restored to her. The final stage began when Grace was able to assume primary control of her own healing and the personalities began to merge. She learned she had authority over the emerging personalities and found that she once again could function in society.

---

[14] James G. Friesen, Uncovering the Mystery of MPD, Here's Life Publishers inc, San Bernardino, CA 1991

3.1.1 Initial stage

To begin the psychological healing, Grace needed to: 1) obtain a basic understanding of her issues; 2) establish emotional pathways that would allow long-buried memories and emotions to escape Grace's subconscious; 3) develop psychological rules that would keep her safe during the healing; and 4) allow new personalities to emerge.

Each of these ran contrary to the mind control; overcoming her programmed opposition was difficult and made this healing phase the most dangerous for Grace. The cult programming had left deeply-embedded suicide traps, set to be triggered by any attempt at accessing subconscious information. Upon realizing that Grace was dealing with satanic ritual abuse, the therapists and medical personnel changed their approach rather significantly and became much more cautious and attuned to the need for spiritual healing. Grace's safe passage through this dangerous initial healing phase would not have been possible if the Holy Spirit had not been present to guide the healers as well as Grace and myself.

Revealing the abuse

When Grace first went into the hospital, we had no idea that she was dealing with satanic ritual abuse. I knew that both her parents and siblings had unusual personalities and were often unpleasant, but I never once suspected the heavy involvement with Satanism and crime. It was during this first hospitalization that the first clues of the satanic ritual abuse began emerging. In light of the severity, the medical team immediately made arrangements for a private room, a setting that would be safer for Grace and one that would not put a roommate at risk.

The no talk rule was so strongly programmed into Grace that it suppressed most of her memories and emotions. However, it was possible to bypass this rule using nonverbal activities such as

Psychological Healing

drawing. Art therapy is a common tool used for releasing emotions and Grace had daily drawing sessions in the hospital. The first definite clues of ritual abuse were illustrated by Grace's drawings of teardrops representing sorrow and red blotches and droplets representing blood.

It was during her first hospitalization that Grace participated in non-dominant hand writing exercises that indicated the multiplicity. She would find her hand writing unusual messages ("You are a monster!"). Names would then begin forming in Grace's consciousness, names that belonged to emerging personalities.

Disturbing dreams and nightmares were another nonverbal clue. These had started some time before and intensified during her hospitalization. The nightmares released long-suppressed memories of abuse, along with pent-up emotions. The memories occasionally occurred during her waking moments. I remember Grace once seeing blood on a doorknob. (There was no physical blood, of course; she was reliving a bloody memory that had invaded her conscious mind.)

The dreams were particularly severe when demonic beings invaded and amplified Grace's feelings of terror. It took spiritual intervention by Grace and the Holy Spirit to end these nightmares. They were not common, but they were traumatic experiences, harbingers of the spiritual healing that would be necessary.

Establishing release pathways

The artwork riddled with themes of blood, along with the nightmares and dreams, were significant clues that Grace was dealing with satanic ritual abuse. But we needed more definitive evidence of the ritual abuse. This was accomplished when hypnotic therapy provided, in a single session, definitive evidence of Grace's involvement with Satanism. In hindsight, while there were two or three pivotal events that propelled her healing to new levels, hypnosis was the first.

Hypnotism

There are many misconceptions about hypnotism, especially within Christian communities for whom hypnotism is viewed as inherently evil. To counter this view, I will describe in some detail the role of hypnotism in Grace's healing. Used correctly, hypnotism was absolutely essential for Grace's healing.

Hypnotism is a neutral technique that can serve either good or evil purposes. Because it was used by the cults to program Grace for evil purposes, hypnotism turned out to be the best tool to begin undoing the evil. It was the hypnosis administered for good that first pierced through cult programming and established a beachhead for healing in Grace's mind. It was hypnosis that provided Grace's first recollections of people dressed in black robes holding a satanic ritual. With the initial information released, the healing efforts shifted from accessing the festering emotions to controlling the rate at which the memories were being released from Grace's subconscious.

Hypnosis not only established a pathway to Grace's subconscious mind--it also opened her subconscious mind to the Holy Spirit. It was therefore the beginning of both the psychological and the spiritual healing. During the hypnosis session, Grace sensed a red glowing presence deep in her subconscious mind. (Red was not a color denoting any form of goodness or godliness.) Her therapist—a Christian--requested the Holy Spirit's presence in Grace's mind. The red glowing presence was joined by a stronger, white glowing presence that was a manifestation of the Holy Spirit's presence.

The hypnotherapy was a one-time event for Grace. But its power unlocked the buried feelings and memories that had been festering in Grace's subconscious. For example, while under hypnosis Grace remembered people dressed in black robes holding a candle light ritual and engaging in abusive behavior. For the first time, we had concrete evidence of the satanic ritual abuse. One of the key goals, uncovering and understanding the nature of Grace's abuse, was accomplished.

The first two goals of the initial psychological healing stage, understanding the nature of the abuse and establishing pathways for the release of feelings and information, had now been established. For the remainder of the healing process, it became more a matter of dealing with and controlling the rate at which these feelings and information emerged. Helping greatly in this process was the administration of medications; especially antidepressant and anti psychotic medications prescribed by a psychiatrist. These drugs effectively prevented the released feelings and information from overwhelming Grace. Having a psychiatrist on Grace's healing team was absolutely essential for her well being.

Rules for healing

As soon as Grace's memories began emerging, it was essential to establish psychological rules and guidelines for safety. These rules addressed suicidal tendencies, self-destructive behavior, flashbacks and helping new personalities.

Suicide prevention: As the difficult and painful memories began to emerge, one obvious but wrong way to mute the memories was though suicide. Understanding this, Grace's therapist had Grace sign a contract promising not to commit suicide; she agreed to call for help if she had suicidal urges. This established a reliable lifeline when needed and gave Grace the responsibility for self-preservation.

This contract became a basic principle of living for Grace, without which, I suspect, she would not be alive today. The urge to commit suicide was so strong that there were days when Grace literally sat on her hands. This prevented using her hands to cut herself with the kitchen knives. There was also one instance when, shortly before being discharged from the hospital, a voice inside her head commanded Grace to kill herself and, furthermore, instructed her how to do it when she got home. This voice may have been demonic or could have been a suicide trap programmed into a personality and triggered if cult information was released. It was the contract that prompted Grace to immediately tell the hospital staff of these suicide plans. Grace's hospitalization was extended a week giving her the time to deal with this issue.

There were occasions when the suicide prevention contract was irrelevant. This happened when Grace, as the host personality, was completely absent and her body's actions were determined solely by a new personality. The danger now was that this new personality had not signed the suicide prevention contract and, indeed, had no knowledge of it. In these cases, suicide prevention required immediate action, such as the "dress for a life" bargain mentioned earlier.

Grace often struggled with self-destructive urges that fell short of suicide. Released emotions and memories were so painful that she would sometimes strike her head with her fists in an attempt to divert the emotional pain into something more manageable. A better technique of pain diversion—one taught to Grace in the hospital--was placing bags of ice on the arms. The cold was just uncomfortable enough to mute the remembered pain without hurting her body.

Flashbacks: Grace's suppressed memories often emerged as sudden, vivid flashbacks in which Grace or one of her personalities would re-live the initial painful experiences (including the emotions). For example, several times she had flashbacks of labor and childbirth. The pain was real, and would often accompany the emergence of new personalities. I frequently found myself as an observer, feeling useless as Grace withered in pain. It seemed the only way she could heal was to experience the flashbacks and break the power of the memories. The rule for healing in this circumstance was simply to let Grace relive the experience while constantly reminding her that she now lived in a different time and place. We have since found out about and have utilized new techniques--rapid eye movement, for example--that enable abuse victims to more rapidly process memories.

The rapid eye movement therapy is formally labeled eye movement desensitization and reprocessing (EMDR)[15] and is a new, nontraditional type of psychotherapy. It is growing in popularity, particularly for treating post-traumatic stress disorder (PTSD). This therapy does not rely on talk therapy or medications. Instead EMDR uses a patient's own rapid, rhythmic eye movements. These eye movements dampen the power of emotionally charged memoires of past traumatic events. Grace has found this therapy to be useful and we both wish that it was available in Grace's initial stages of healing.

Helping new personalities: If the discovery of Grace's past involvement with Satanism was a surprise, the multiple personality disorder (MPD) was a shock. We progressed from the early hints (as dramatic mood shifts) to more startling evidence (as when she saw some one else in a mirror). Soon the emergence of new personalities was a regular occurrence. (We found that the great majority of Grace's personalities were children; the shock felt by the emerging personality was typically strong enough to penetrate Grace's conscious mind and leave her with, for example, the unexplained feeling of seeing someone else in the mirror.)

It was not long after Grace's first hospitalization that I began talking to the new personalities. This experience was unnerving at first; I had to quickly learn to suppress any feelings of revulsion during the most uncomfortable conversations. It is now routine for me to talk with a variety of different people, each speaking with my wife's voice and sharing her body.

---

[15] A. Tan, M. Salgado, S. Fahn. Movement Disorders. Wiley Online Library, 1996

It was crucial to establish basic rules as the personalities emerged. The first, and most important, rule was that Grace was host personality and had authority over the others. This kept her responsible for her own actions and prevented personality chaos that could eventually lead to full-blown psychosis. We implemented this rule simply by making sure each new personality knew that Grace was the boss. This was so effective that alternate personalities, after their initial orientation, would simply refer to 'boss Grace' during our conversations.

In the intermediate healing stage, this principle was challenged several times by dominant personalities; for example, there was one particular personality that seemed to have night-time governing status that was almost equivalent to that of Grace in the day time. With some convincing, she agreed to step down and submit to Grace's authority. (This personality had functioned as a priestess for the cult, hence her night-time dominance.)

It was important for emerging personalities to voice their feelings, thoughts and opinions, thereby encouraging their complete and full emergence from Grace's subconscious. This enabled them to be engaged in the present, preventing them from retreating into past memories. There was no attempt to suppress the emergence of new personalities no matter how uncomfortable or inconvenient the emerging process was. I am convinced that this philosophy of openness was healthy, although I did need to take care to ensure that Grace, as the host personality, was always recognized and accepted.

3.1.2 Intermediate stage

The initial stage took almost a year: The satanic origins of her abuse were now known, and the barriers that suppressed memories had been pierced. We had also established a framework for keeping Grace safe and sane as she began to manage the

Psychological Healing

multiple personality disorder. She was now ready for the next stage.

The intermediate stage required several more hospitalizations and lasted several years; it was during this time that the majority of the deprogramming took place. Hundreds of personalities began emerging, each with its own terrible memories; Grace and I struggled to keep up. Daily struggles with new personalities (and the demons possessing them) became routine. I remember days when three or four new personalities would emerge; each requiring at least a half hour—some a full hour--to help.

I remember one day when the Holy Spirit, brought a kind of spiritual dump truck—that was how Grace described it-- to pick up all the Holy Spirit bags containing demons being removed from new personalities. This routine seemed to go on and on without a let up for several years. By the end of it, Grace and I—along with the medical team--had helped over a thousand new personalities escape their psychological prisons. A legion of demons had been removed from Grace.

This stage left us physically, mentally and spiritually exhausted—but never completely overwhelmed. It was just a process that, with the help of the Holy Spirit and wise and caring medical professionals, steadily proceeded until Grace's personalities were released and freed from Satan's clutches.

Psychological tools

This stage required its own special psychological tools. The first stage had centered on safety—suicide prevention—and the signing of a contract. Now Grace needed to learn how to communicate directly with her personalities. This kept Grace sane throughout the healing process, especially with the emergence of so many new personalities. When communicating with them, she also needed to offer them a refuge in her mind—a safe place from which they could begin the re-integration process.

Inner communication: As personalities emerged, they would communicate with me or with Grace's therapist. Since an hour was usually insufficient to really help a personality, I assumed most of the responsibility for communicating with Grace's personalities. I soon found myself spending hours talking with personalities, playing an intermediary role between Grace and her personalities. This placed me under a lot of stress; more importantly, it undermined Grace's authority.

Surprisingly, this arrangement proceeded for over a year before reaching a crisis situation. One day, several personalities simply refused to give Grace the control over her body--I came home from work to find Grace on the floor able only to crawl. There was a battle going on in her mind for the executive control over her body. This was not a spiritual battle. Instead it was a battle of "minds" within Grace. She checked into the hospital and, after a single hour long session with a specialist, learned to communicate with her inner personalities. She now had the ability to truly become the host personality and slowly lead her personality system towards good mental health. This represented a turning point in her psychological healing, one that was as significant as the initial hypnotherapy.

This event points out several important aspects of the deprogramming process. First, the episode was mainly caused by inadequate psychotherapy. Grace's therapist, at the time, was working with the personalities more than with Grace herself. (The therapist wisely realized her inexperience and referred Grace to a more qualified therapist.) With hindsight, I now realize that a therapist and caregiver should always work chiefly with the main or host personality. Grace's personality system needed the leadership and authority of a strong host personality. By working almost exclusively with the personalities, the authority of the host personality was being undermined.

We soon found that a healthy host personality can better help the personalities as they emerge from their subconscious, "sleeping" states. Grace, as the host personality, needed to be enabled and encouraged to take authority over her mind and personalities. Grace's newfound authority relieved me of the responsibility to help each new personality; the responsibility for self care was placed where it belonged, with Grace.

This turned out to be an important part of the deprogramming since, in the cult, individual responsibility and care giving were suppressed and each person was controlled by superiors. Each, in turn, was then expected to control inferiors in the cult hierarchy. Without the tool of inner communication with her personalities, each personality would tend to revert to the cult programming and have little hope for healing.

Inner communication enabled Grace to manage and understand her personality system. For example, when a younger personality got frightened, Grace was now able to immediately provide words of comfort. But inner communication was much more than mere verbal communications; feelings and, to some degree, visual communication were equally important. In some cases, young frightened personalities were not be able to articulate their fears but with practice Grace found that she could sense the fear and offer comfort much as one would offer comfort to the unspoken fears of a young child.

There have been times when her inner vision—the ability to see what the personalities see--has been crucial. For example, at one point in her healing, Grace felt that something was wrong. Upon checking inside her mind, Grace "saw" personalities sitting in circles with candles; they apparently were regressing toward cult-like behavior. Grace was able to disband the group and correct the inner misbehavior. Without this ability to "see" her personality system, the dangerous behavior would likely have continued unchecked.

The safe place house: As the personalities emerged from Grace's subconscious, they needed a place to go within Grace's mind that was under her control and out of danger. We called this haven the safe place house, established with a therapist's help and guidance; it was, in essence, a tool to break the cult control of Grace's mind, restoring it to wholeness under the nurturing of the Holy Spirit. This was a place where personalities could safely rest, communicate with Grace and begin the merging process (This will be described later in this chapter). Personalities, with Grace's permission, were free to come forward from the safe place house, into Grace's consciousness, and experience reality directly. They were no longer trapped and hidden somewhere in Grace's subconscious.

The safe place house began as a simple dwelling in which her personalities could live safely as they were rescued from bondage in other locations of Grace's unconscious. As more personalities emerged and began integrating, the house grew in size and sophistication. It eventually became more of a hotel or resort than a single house, structured to conform to the needs of the personalities. It contained dormitory style rooms as well as some private bedrooms and study areas for individual personalities. One room—designed for a studiously inclined personality who was a former cult priestess--was lined with books from floor to ceiling. There was also a loft area for the boy personalities that opened into a balcony from which star-gazing could be done with a telescope. The loft contained other outdoors orientated items such as hammocks and camping supplies. The grounds surrounding the safe place house were also instrumental in helping personalities. For example, there was a large tree providing shade under which

Psychological Healing

younger personalities sat on the grass and listened to a Holy Spirit angel reading stories such as Winnie the Pooh.

I do not know whether the safe place house was purely imaginary or whether it was rooted in a spiritual reality. Grace could see it so, in practice, I treated it as a real place; it was indeed the place where a great deal of real spiritual and psychological healing took place. In this way it was a foretaste of heaven for personalities who had endured so much; hearing Grace's description makes me more eager than ever for that final safe place house that God promised he has prepared for us.

The safe place house also was a kind of holding area for the newest personalities. It could take months, sometimes years, for personalities to become acclimated with Grace's present reality. The security of the safe place house ensured that personalities did not simply disappear back into the subconscious.

Grace's father had also given Grace's personalities a place to stay in her mind—a place to which only he and other cult members had access and control. An important part of the deprogramming required moving personalities from the father's control area in Grace's subconscious mind into Grace's control area, the safe place house.

The system: As new personalities began occupying the safe place house, it became necessary to organize these personalities. Certain key personalities assumed leadership roles within the safe place house and began working with Grace. In this way Grace effectively became the chairperson presiding over a board comprised of these dominant personalities. The remaining personalities were organized under this board. We called this ensemble of personalities "the system"; new personalities were integrated into this system upon emergence from Grace's subconscious mind.

This system of personalities became a powerful and positive force. For example, there were times when Grace simply became too fatigued for day-to-day operation and the system took over temporarily while Grace rested. With better access to Grace's subconscious, the system was not only instrumental in helping new personalities as they emerged, but eventually began advance preparations for new personalities who had not yet emerged. I suspect that the system has also helped in ways that I am not aware.

With the tools of inner communication, the safe place house and the personality system established, Grace's healing and deprogramming proceeded quickly. Now the key issue became controlling the rate at which the memories, feelings and personalities emerged. Anti-psychotic and anti-depressive drugs, hospitalizations and plenty of psychotherapy were all necessary for this stage.

Multiple Personalities

The goal of the deprogramming was breaking the cult's control over Grace's mind and transferring control back to Grace. This was accomplished through three steps: 1) accessing Grace's personalities; 2) freeing them from satanic bondage; and 3) welcoming them back into that portion of Grace's mind under her control. As this process proceeded, the cult control over Grace's mind continued to shrink as fewer and fewer personalities were left who were under cult control via the programming.

As part of the healing process, Grace's reasoning abilities and value system slowly straightened out. Before the healing, her thinking was often convoluted due to the influence of personalities deeply infected with Satan's value system. This was especially noticeable in a religious context, where a passage of scripture or a pastor's sermon intended for comfort would be twisted into a destructive message driving Grace to self destructive tendency. Liberating these personalities not only accomplished the

Psychological Healing

deprogramming but also contributed greatly to righting Grace's reasoning abilities

Over a period of several years, many new personalities emerged. I initially tried to keep a record of the name of each new personality and keep a running count of the total. But after hundreds of new personalities, I finally abandoned any attempt to keep track of all the names. And after a thousand personalities had emerged, I even lost interest in keeping a running count. The staggering level of abuse had fractured her mind into thousands of pieces, and complete healing required that all these pieces needed to be carefully fitted back together.

The Holy Spirit was clearly the leader in this tremendous effort. He chose which personalities should emerge and when they should awake. He was not just there for the removal of demons— He also guided us in navigating a tricky and sometimes dangerous deprogramming process. Because of this, and with the tremendous help of a skilled medical team, Grace has healed from the satanic ritual abuse and her mind has been restored from the years of programming.

The core of the deprogramming effort was assimilating each new personality into the system of personalities under Grace's control. The details varied according to need and changed significantly over the several year course of healing. But the general pattern was the emergence, initiation, integration and maintenance for each new personality. These will be described in detail in the following sections.

Emergence

Controlling the rate and manner at which personalities emerged became a balance between the risk of full-blown psychosis (in which Grace could be overwhelmed by too many personalities emerging in a very short period of time) and the practical matter of helping over a thousand personalities. It was fortunate that in the early stages I had no idea there would be so many personalities--that knowledge would have been completely demoralizing for both of us.

Prescription anti-psychotic drugs aided greatly in this process; they kept Grace mentally stable and reduced the overwhelming sensations and feelings as the personalities emerged. But I think that the work of the Holy Spirit was the key ingredient; during this time, Grace sometimes reported seeing internal barrack-like buildings containing rows of beds with sleeping personalities. The Holy Spirit would walk down aisles awakening those personalities ready for this transition. He not only controlled the emergence rate but also selected the order of awakening. This order was important since the emergence of a personality with extraordinarily difficult issues was always draining for Grace; two personalities with severe issues waking up in close succession to each other could be overwhelming.

The initial signs that a new personality was emerging varied significantly. A sudden change in behavior--irritability or sudden fear, for example—was sometimes an indication that Grace's emotions were beginning to overlap with those of an awaking personality. The outpouring of emotions being released by memories of abuse would disturb Grace even before she had any understanding of their origin. The emotions were sometimes strong enough to interfere with bodily functions, especially if a baby or very young child was emerging. In such cases Grace might suddenly have an unsteady gait, almost as if she were intoxicated.

With experience, I was able to sense slight changes in mannerisms—a different expression or a blank stare was a telltale sign. An emerging personality seeing through Grace's eyes for the first time would sometimes stare at me and ask who are you? Each emerging personality needed to be introduced to me and to Grace in order to begin the healing process.

Psychological Healing

Sometimes personalities woke up in groups of two or three. When this happened, I often was not aware of it until I heard a new voice asking 'what about me?' or 'can I come too?' These combinations of personalities usually carried different emotions connected to the same memory; if the abuse was severe enough it took more than one personality to fully contain the feelings. When this happened, I simply treated each personality separately and helped each personality one at a time.

Initiation

I had no formal psychological training for this type of therapy, but with so many emerging personalities, the chances of effective treatment during the therapist's allotted time were slim. It did not help that the particular issues of the personalities varied tremendously. The good news was that with some patience, common sense and guidance from the Holy Spirit, I was able to successfully help all the new personalities. In the most difficult cases I was able to provide just enough help for Grace to manage without harm until she could meet with the therapist.

The initial challenge was to bring new personalities to a point where they could comprehend and accept their new situation. I was, in essence, initiating them into a whole new life. In those moments, the most important message was you are safe and this is a new time and a new place. This was not a magic phrase—it took time and patience to convince personalities that they were indeed safe from harm. With this message communicated, each new personality could be assimilated into Grace's personality system. I developed a kind of spiritual and psychological procedure to do this. The spiritual part of this process has been described in detail; I will now describe the detailed psychological process.

As Grace's personality system matured, the system itself began initiating personalities even before emergence. For example, many emerging personalities distrusted my intent; most of them had only known abusive men and it was natural that I was considered with great suspicion and fear. I would sometimes spend hours talking with a new personality before gaining her or his trust enough to be helpful. As Grace's personality system matured the system began persuading new personalities about to emerge that I was safe and trustworthy. In that way I was eventually able to spend more time helping without a long and difficult period of building trust.

Difficult issues

As I describe the process of helping emerging personalities, I will begin by describing some of the most difficult cases. These emerged before I had gained very much experience in helping personalities and before Grace's system had matured enough to be helpful. I nonetheless persisted and, with the Holy Spirit's help and guidance, was able to help even these difficult personalities.

There were usually telltale signs of especially severe issues. I became especially sensitive to any indication that the emerging personality might be a boy or baby. The emergence of a baby personality was fairly obvious—she would make baby sounds and cause Grace's legs and arms to buckle and flail about just like the movement of a baby or very young child.

The main problem with baby personalities was the difficulty of communication. These personalities could be integrated only after Grace began developing her own inner communication skills; with Grace as an intermediary, I could begin helping the babies.

Boy or boyish personalities were more difficult to detect. It was usually not obvious until the new personality objected to being called a girl or was hesitant about being called a girl. In my experience, boy personalities always had the most severe issues; they seemed to be the holders of the most graphic 'blood

Psychological Healing

and guts' type of memories. I believe that the reason why they formed as boy personalities was a perception that, as a boy, they were better suited to handle the more severe abuse. This pattern was so consistent that I would brace myself for some especially disgusting memories whenever a boy was emerging. On the other hand, once such personalities had been helped they added a lot of strength, both physical and mental, to Grace's personality system.

The only personality that I had no success in helping was a boy that was renamed Josiah. (My encounter with Josiah is described at the beginning of the spiritual healing chapter.) In this case, I spent over an hour trying to help this personality with no success. His psychological issues were so deeply intertwined with spiritual issues (common for many of Grace's personalities) that it required direct intervention by the Holy Spirit and Jesus Christ. Josiah has never needed any more help since.

Personalities sometimes emerged experiencing body memories. If a personality had formed in the midst of an especially abusive experience, upon waking they were still in that memory and feeling the abuse just as though it was still happening. Examples of these body memories included an ear ache caused by a blow to Grace's head with a pipe, hand pain caused by the bite of a poisonous spider, abdomen pains caused by blows to the body and vaginal tenderness caused by rape. These body memories were so real that I remember seeing Grace's hand turn red and irritated when remembering the poisonous spider bite on her hand.

I never found a better way of helping Grace through these body memories other than simply being with her and waiting for the memory to work itself out. (There are now new psychotherapy techniques that can help to ease body memories. These involve rapid eye movement and seem to enable a rapid and more controlled release of these body memories.) Whether simply through time, or through special therapy, these personalities needed to work through their body memory before being initiated into the new life. The body memory represented abuse that needed cleansing and releasing before a personality could completely live in the present.

Childbirth produced the most severe body memories. These occurred several times and were extremely painful for Grace and shocking for both of us. It was extraordinary to see Grace's abdomen swell just as if she were pregnant; her body would strain in pain as a woman in labor. In these episodes, she was reliving memories of her role as a forced 'breeder' (described in the abuse chapter), in which the babies, when delivered, became human sacrifices.

As mentioned in the abuse chapter, the cults used young girls, often pre-teens, as "breeders." These girls would be impregnated and then the babies, when delivered, became sacrificial food. The case of Grace's 'bathroom delivery' (described in the abuse chapter) was so severe that it required three personalities to contain the memories and emotions. (Each of these personalities had a name starting with the latter M, so I would call these personalities the 3Ms). They emerged with intense body memories that rendered them extraordinarily weak, just as with a sudden loss of blood. When introduced to Grace's personality system, they rested and recovered in the safe place house. Grace's recovery from this experience took several days, but the complete healing of the 3Ms took several years of rest in the safe place house.

There were other personalities with body memories just as extreme as the 3Ms mentioned above. While Grace's body had recovered from the physical abuse long before, the memories of this abuse had been stored and needed healing. And, as far as these emerging personalities were concerned, the abuse was both real and current.

In extreme cases--such as the 3Ms--extreme action needed to be taken. This was one of the areas where the spiritual and psychological healing often overlapped. For the most difficult cases, I found it essential to ask the Holy Spirit to give the blood of Jesus Christ to an injured personality. When the personality drank Christ's blood (done on a spiritual level, of course); the blood became cool, healing and refreshing water that gave new energy and healing to that personality. If the blood was used to wash a wound, the blood became a healing rinse for the personality and the wound was healed.

I don't know exactly how to interpret the administration of Christ's blood, except that it provided real healing power to physical pain being experienced by the personalities. Most important, it enabled the healing of personalities in situations that were beyond the help of ordinary therapy or routine exorcism. The blood of Christ healed emotions as well. One personality felt intense guilt for actions she had been forced into as a child. Her hands had committed violent acts and were stained with the horror and guilt of what she had done. As the blood of Christ poured over her hands, the feelings were released and she saw the red stain on her hands cleansed in forgiveness.

A personality's response to healing, whether of a physical wound or an emotional wound, was usually an outburst of joy. I remember a wonderful moment of healing when a personality— one who had been very sick--got up after drinking Christ's blood from a vial and started dancing with Christ. This expression of joy was heartwarming; I am glad that the God I serve was willing to dance, hand in hand, with a little girl.

There were several instances of new personalities who did not speak English or could communicate only by writing, often writing in a language that was clearly not English and in an unfamiliar script. I remember one personality who wrote several pages entirely in a script that looked like Arabic. I had no way of communicating with the personality directly, but there was another personality who acted as an interpreter so the necessary inner work could be done.

As Grace's healing progressed fewer personalities emerged with these kinds of severe issues. They now seemed to be aware of the new time and circumstances, and there eventually became little distinction between a new personality and a one who had been awake for a much longer time. This created a new round of difficulties, because emerging personalities were not so obvious. However, whenever I found myself talking to a personality who was overly upset or fearful, I would take that as a clue that a new personality was emerging. I found that a good test was to ask the personality if she or he knew my name, and especially if she had a Holy Spirit angel friend. Non-committal answers were a clear indication that I was talking to a new personality who needed immediate help.

Integration

Once initiated, new personalities were ready for integration into Grace's personality system. In this, the ultimate goal was the rebuilding of Grace's mind. I often think of Grace's mind as a beautiful plate that had been purposely dropped, shattering into many pieces. The largest piece was Grace herself, but each smaller piece represented a vital part of her personality. The integration process allows each piece to rejoin the plate, with the ultimate goal of a complete plate with its original beauty.

Other important integration goals included safety, retention and comfort. If isolated, a personality state was subject to demonic oppression and potential control by cult members. Integration into Grace's personality system brought personalities directly under Grace's authority and under the watchful eye of the Holy Spirit angels who have been given permission to protect the personalities.

Also, the integration prevented personalities from slipping back into a sleeping mode; essentially disappearing back into Grace's unconsciousness. The key goal of Grace's healing was exposing issues and memories so they could be dealt with. This meant not only bringing personalities out of Grace's subconscious mind but keeping them out of their initial subconscious, slumber like states so their memories and experiences could be exposed and healed.

Integration Methods

The key steps in integrating new personalities into Grace's personality system were 1) transfer to the safe place house, 2) giving personalities a variety of helpful items and 3) giving each new personality rules for living in the safe place house. Of course, these steps varied somewhat according to the specific needs of new personalities and Grace.

Transfer: Spiritual healing was really the first stage of integration. It removed any demons attached to new personalities, introduced each new personality to God, and provided Holy Spirit angels for each personality. With this accomplished, I could transfer new personalities into Grace's safe place house without worry that demons would compromise the healing.

It was vitally important that these personalities have somewhere to go for care and protection. Thus, the safe place house became an important part of the integration process. Grace had complete access to it, it was filled with Holy Spirit angels for protection and it was a comfortable place for nurturing and living. Most of the personalities living in the safe place house eventually became entirely integrated with Grace's personality. This was the ultimate goal of the healing process. I will describe this merging process later in this chapter.

Some personalities were reluctant to transfer, since change of any kind—especially for personalities with memories of abuse—was difficult. To make this change easier, I would usually explain what was going to happen and describe the benefits of transferring to the safe place house. I would also emphasize that the move would be from one portion of the mind to another portion of the mind, assuring the personality that they would not get lost in the process. This was usually sufficient to encourage personalities to transfer but occasionally a new personality still refused the transfer. For these cases, I found it useful to give the personality a glimpse into the safe place house. After seeing the beautiful grounds and the other child personalities playing, they were almost always excited to make the change. Using these approaches, Grace and I have never had a severe problem in transfer; once the transfer was completed, we have never encountered a personality's request to leave the safe place house. It has been a wonderful tool for psychological healing.

Specificity about the destination was always important when making a transfer. Without this, the personality could end up in an unknown subconscious location or demonic stronghold and be lost. Also, the spiritual work done prior to this transfer gave each personality a Holy Spirit angel. It was important to specify that each personality's Holy Spirit angel also be transferred along with that personality to the safe place house.

Infant or toddler personalities required more care and were transferred to a special nursery section of the safe place house. For infants it was clear that they needed to be transferred to this nursery area but for toddlers the appropriate section of the safe place house for transfer was sometimes uncertain. The toddler personality was often given the preview of the safe place house nursery to assess their preference. Typically, their decision was based on the type of toys present in the nursery area.

Once personalities were transferred to the safe place house, they were given gifts, mentors and rules to live by. Along with the transfer itself, these actions represented the completion of the deprogramming. Personalities were now freed from cult and demonic bondage and integrated into a personality system that was under Grace's authority.

Gifts: When transferred into the safe place house, each personality was given 'inside' items such as a bed, toys and clothing articles. These and other possessions were gifts that established the personalities in their new lives with Grace, demonstrated each one's importance, and gave them a sense of belonging. These items were tailored to their needs and wishes. For example, many personalities had been abused in beds so having a safe bed was important. For a bed to be safe, it sometimes simply needed to be different from the one Grace had grown up with. In other cases, a safe bed was a bed decorated with butterflies or painted a particular color.

Next, each personality was given a memory book and memory box for memories both good and bad. When particular memories needed to be processed, the associated personality just took the memory out of the memory book or box. If the memory box became too heavy, each personality's Holy Spirit angel carried it. While not physical items, they were nevertheless very real tools for Grace's healing.

In addition to the memory book and box, all new personalities were given an internal 'book of the common knowledge of the system' for reading. This book was essentially a history of Grace's life. By reading this, each personality better understood how they related to Grace. Since the personalities had been asleep for decades, the book also helped bridge the gap between the present and past.

As the personalities woke up, Grace and I wanted them to have a strong connection with the present. What better way to do this than to enable them to see through Grace's eyes even when they were in the safe place house? So we set up a virtual television in the safe place house that showed the outside world as seen by Grace. (This television or monitor was a shared possession.) Grace could turn off the monitor at her discretion. This would be appropriate, for example, when viewing certain movies since nearly all the personalities were children. This internal television also served a dual purpose. As each new personality was transferred to the safe place house, that personality was required to watch a welcoming video so that personalities who had been asleep for decades could receive information about Grace and her current life.

As part of the transfer process, each new personality was given a mentor—an experienced personality--who also lived in the safe place house. The mentor was a well-adjusted personality who had been awake for some time. The mentor would immediately talk with the newly arrived personality, establishing inner communication between personalities, providing comfort, and giving information about Grace's personality system. Grace and I did not specifically pick out mentors but simply asked that the personality system itself select a personality appropriate to the task.

Rules: The transfer process was complete when each new personality understood the rules by which order was established and maintained within Grace's personality system. This ensured everyone's safety and comforted those newcomers unsure of their new surroundings.

The first--and most important—rule was that Grace was the boss. This established Grace's authority, since it was essential that there be only one head of the personality system. Since most of the personalities were accustomed to a strong hierarchical cult structure, this rule was usually accepted. Sometimes, as in the case of the night-time priestess, the personality needed some convincing.

Psychological Healing

Because Grace was the boss (she was often referred to as Boss Grace), it followed that personalities must no longer obey Grace's mother, father, or any demons. Their allegiance needed a radical shift from evil to Boss Grace and, ultimately, the Holy Spirit. This was part of the basic deprogramming strategy of shifting authority away from the cults to Grace. I often encountered resistance to this rule. Personalities were justifiably afraid that Grace's father would be angry; it was important to assure them that they would be safe and that they no longer lived under the authority of their father.

Despite Grace's authority, there was always some danger of self-inflicted pain and suicide; this was even stronger during the most intense healing. To counter this, we established a no-hurting rule that began with her no-suicide pledge to the therapist: Personalities were told that they must not hurt Grace's body or any other personalities, in any way. In this way, each new personality became a new 'signatory', agreeing to the pledge that Grace had originally made. I cannot overstate the importance of this rule. Adherence to the no-hurting rule has prevented self-inflicted abuse and even suicide.

The helping rule was the positive instruction given to complement the no-hurting rule. It was essential for Grace's personalities to begin taking responsibility in caring for the physical and emotional needs of their body. For example, nutrition, exercise and sleep are all vital to self-care. Since much of the abuse occurred at night (Grace was often called for rituals by a sudden night-time awakening), the personalities often stayed awake simply out of fear. As a result, sleeping through the night has been a consistent issue for Grace. It became a bedtime ritual to assure, and reassure Grace's personalities that there would be no hurting during the night. Our bedtime routine included stories read just before sleeping time and, if a personality still would not sleep, Grace and I would sometimes let personalities stay awake and rest in the safe place house while the body slept through the night.

I learned to be very careful when suggesting that a personality go to sleep. For some personalities this suggestion was interpreted as an instruction to disappear into Grace's unconscious. (Their concept of sleep was not an overnight sleep but rather one of unconsciousness until being wakened by a cult member.) Careless words could undo the work of transferring a personality into Grace's personality system and safe place house. In cases like this, the ability, and willingness, of personalities to voice their concerns would often alert me before a mistake like that was made.

Another major rule was the no sex rule. Only personalities that were age twenty-one or older and were married to me qualified for intimate sexual relations. Personalities who were too young or not yet ready went to their places in Grace's safe place house during times of sexual intimacy.

This rule existed first to protect the sanctity of marriage. The outburst of emotions from memories of abuse could easily interrupt our most intimate moments. The rule also assured personalities that they would not be harmed. Most of the younger personalities associated sexual intimacy with pain because of the real pain they had experienced in the abuse. As a result, it was not difficult to exempt personalities from sexual activity; they were usually relieved.

It was important for new personalities who were older and beginning to merge to know that they were married. Our solution, at least during the early and middle healing stages, was to have personalities participate in a marriage ceremony with a minister. In the latter healing stage, merging enabled a full understanding of marriage, including sexual intimacy, without needing to go through a marriage ceremony.

Psychological Healing

There were a number of other rules for the personalities to follow. One of these was that only Boss Grace takes medicine. The physiology of Grace's body appeared to change according to who was forward and in executive control of her body. This is one of the bizarre effects of personality disorder. For example, I remember one morning when a younger personality was forward and was excitedly jumping and running in a friend's yard. This personality suddenly switched control of the body with Grace. Within seconds, Grace's heartbeat accelerated and Grace became much winded. I do not understand how this happens but apparently the brain exerts an even greater control over the body than modern medical science acknowledges.

Another rule stated that only personalities sixteen years of age or older could help Grace drive the car. I remember vividly one occasion when Grace (I thought), was driving our car into an entrance ramp to a freeway. When I heard her exclaim 'how do we do this?' I quickly figured out that a personality had surfaced who had never driven a car before. Asking the personality to suddenly switch with Grace at that crucial moment would have been quite dangerous; with a racing heart, I coached this personality through her first driving lesson. The traffic was mercifully light that day, and the personality was able to merge onto the freeway uneventfully.

This incident emphasized the importance that Boss Grace needed to be in control; it was especially important that personalities not suddenly surface and take control of the body whenever they wanted to. This could be disruptive for the system, socially embarrassing and physically dangerous. So we established a rule that personalities must get permission from Boss Grace to come forward from the safe place house before any attempt to surface. Problems arose even with this rule in place, especially for new personalities unfamiliar with the rules.

One risk of breaking this rule was a tendency for Grace to bite her tongue or mouth. The transition of personalities taking over body control is never seamless; when body control switched from Boss Grace to a younger personality the timing of mouth action was often disrupted and triggered a bite reflex. Grace's tongue has been bitten many times, a painful irritant that is still an issue today.

Many personalities were specifically trained in the use of knives for cutting flesh. Considering the suicidal tendencies of many emerging personalities, this knowledge was especially dangerous. Each new personality was therefore given the rule that only Boss Grace could use knives for food preparation. This rule--along with the no-hurt rule--has kept Grace safe, even though there were times when she had to force herself to sit on her hands for hours to keep from going into the kitchen and using knives to cut her wrists. Also as a practical precaution, I always made sure that the kitchen knives were always washed and put away when not in use.

Advanced methods

After almost a decade of learning what was necessary for healing, we began using what I will call advanced healing methods, in which new personalities were given a crash course on integrating into Grace's personality system. There were three steps in the advanced healing methodology: 1) Talking with Boss Grace; 2) Switching places with Boss Grace and 3) Overlapping with Boss Grace. In all three steps, the help of the Holy Spirit was absolutely essential.

The first step--having a new personality speak internally with Boss Grace--ensured good internal communication. Prior to this, new personalities had usually begun talking to other personalities first, and gradually learned to speak with Boss Grace. Teaching the new personality to immediately begin communicating with Boss Grace accelerated the integration process. In a typical scenario, I would ask the new personality to talk with Boss Grace (the 'lady in the head').

The second and third steps were more complicated. Switching places with Grace simply meant that the new personality came to the foreground of consciousness while Grace receded into the background. This allowed me to speak directly to the new personality without the need for Grace. Overlapping with Grace meant that the new personality could sense Grace's feelings and vice a versa. All three steps were challenging for both Grace and a new personality. But all three steps represented a large step forward in Grace's healing process.

While there was some reluctance to participate (new personalities were often afraid of adults), persistence usually convinced the new personality to agree. These methods were also sometimes slowed because of fatigue; Grace was simply too tired to continue helping new personalities after the initial efforts of spiritual and psychological healing already described were completed. However, with the reluctance overcome the steps could be completed at a pace consistent with Grace's energy level.

4. Final stage

With the bulk of the psychological healing accomplished, Grace began the final stage of healing—the merging of personalities with Grace. This began about a decade after the first diagnosis and is ongoing; I suspect that it will continue for the rest of her earthly life. Each new personality must be spiritually free and communicating fully before merging, so the first two stages are continuously being practiced.

Maturation & merging

When personalities were transferred to the safe place house, they began a maturing process. With their release, they would begin aging for the first time, with babies becoming children and children becoming adolescents. The bedtime stories would shift from nursery rhymes to Nancy Drew adventures.

The rate at which personalities aged was independent of the actual time passing; it seemed dependent only on a personality's desire to mature. We saw evidence of this through changing interests, increasing emotional stability and awareness of Grace's feelings and thoughts. Most of the time this process was so gradual and effortless that we were largely unaware of it. I remember one day when Grace checked the safe place house and was alarmed to find that, on several floors, the beds were mostly empty, and there were few children to be found anywhere in the safe place house and on its grounds. She quickly investigated, only to find that they were not missing at all; they had simply merged with her without any fanfare. For these personalities the healing was over and complete. The cult programming was being broken and her mind was being restored one personality at a time.

As the merging has continued, Grace finds herself revisiting past issues, typically arising from emotions previously confined within personalities. After merging these feelings have become Grace's feelings. Many of these are connected to unpleasant memories and require ongoing therapy. Anger towards her mother, who not only allowed the abuse but initiated much of it, has been among the most difficult issues for Grace. I suspect that dealing with these residual feelings will be a continual process during the rest of her life.

As part of the healing, Grace has needed to learn life skills that are normally learned in childhood and adolescence. When growing up, most emotional stress was simply compartmentalized into buried personalities. This was done either by consciously pushing the feelings into a personality or by dissociation. If left unattended and if severe enough, the emotions and suppressed memories would eventually generate a new personality. With the merging process, fewer personalities are available to contain unpleasant feelings; Grace has instead had to master the difficult task of expressing emotions and sharing memories when they arise.

Similarly, it is still a challenge for Grace to handle emotions and memories that seem to surface at one time. In the past, these would be unconsciously delegated to personalities. She is learning instead to manage these challenges 'in parallel', a skill that is very difficult.

5. Costs

This chapter would not be complete without describing the high cost of Grace's healing. The cost was not only financial but, included the loss of many hopes and dreams. For example, at an age when other women are raising families and/or developing careers, Grace was totally consumed by a spiritual and psychological fight for survival. She lost the most productive time of her life to the healing process. Now, after two decades healing, Grace is ready to embark upon her life in the same fashion that a twenty year old might. Except that now, exhausted from years of healing, she lacks the health and energy to do the things she had dreamed of: raising a child, developing her talents and enjoying physical activity. It is sad for me to witness such a waste of talent and potential contribution to society.

Grace's healing would have been impossible without her medical team; there was no substitute for their knowledge and experience, especially during crucial periods of hospitalization. But doctors, hospitals, and therapists make their living by providing services and the resulting medical cost of Grace's treatment was staggering; the aggregate costs approached two hundred thousand dollars (and this was several decades ago). I was thankful to have good medical insurance through my employment, but the lifetime limit for mental health was then fifty thousand dollars. As a result, I was left paying for the bulk of these expenses myself.

The process was indeed expensive, but was entirely worthwhile. Now--a decade later--Grace and I are just recovering financially. But Grace has completed most of the healing and is enjoying her life now. The benefits of the healing will continue for Grace--not only in this life, but, I am also convinced, in the life to come.

6. Key Lessons

When we began the deprogramming, I did not understand what would be required in time, energy and expense; had I known what I now know, I might not have had the courage to proceed. But the effort, drawn out over many years, has been doable with help from therapists, psychiatrists and God's intervention. The first lesson was patience and persistence in the face of a nearly impossible task.

We also learned that God chose not to act destructively towards Grace even though I am convinced that simply destroying some of her memories (along with the cult programming) would have made her life easier and would have hastened the healing process. But memories—even horrific ones—were resident in personalities that are an essential part of Grace's mind. God would not destroy any part of Grace's mind, however small. He desires nothing less than complete healing for Grace. This is what made the psychological healing so much more difficult than the spiritual healing. It is far more difficult to heal a mind twisted by cult programming than it is to exorcise demons. With the help of the Holy Spirit, I was able to use God's power to remove and destroy demons at will.

We also learned the importance of inner communication. Grace needed to communicate directly with her personalities since they were a part of her. She needed unimpeded access to all portions of her mind to be in executive control. This is an ability that every normally functioning person has and is something that I completely take for granted. But it is not automatic for a person subjected to the extreme abuse suffered by Grace.

During the process, I also learned to depend on Grace herself for answers to many otherwise baffling issues. I learned that the answer to a troubling issue would often come from within Grace herself. I found it especially important to resist my own tendency toward problem solving and, instead, ask Grace for the answer. This approach often solved the issue and was affirming for Grace in the long process of regaining executive control of her mind. It enabled her to think and function independently of others, in stark contrast to the cult training.

Early on in the healing, Grace and I learned that her situation was so extreme that ordinary Christians simply could not identify with our challenges and were prone to shunning us when perceiving our difficulties. As a result, much of Grace's deprogramming has been done in isolation from the church body of Christian believers. Reactions like this are understandable; were I in their shoes, not knowing what I now know, I might have reacted as they did.

Nevertheless, I challenge believers and the churches to be more accepting of those going through the extreme spiritual and psychological battles that Grace and I have experienced. A simple smile and word of encouragement is wonderful when in the depths of struggles with the enemy. The reward of embracing people like us with tolerance and God's grace is worth the risk. Learning of what God has done to save Grace from Satan's clutches could be tremendously encouraging for ordinary Christians. What could possibly be more comforting than the image of Christ dancing hand in hand with a small child such as one of Grace's personalities who had just been released from slavery to Satan and the psychological bondage of cult programming?

7. Summary

The bulk of the psychological healing has taken nearly twenty years. The battle for control of Grace's mind has been fought one personality at a time, often at great risk. We estimate that over a thousand personalities have been released from their imprisonment and transferred to the safe place house. Many of these have merged with Grace and their healing has been completed. Yet there still remain more personalities in the merging process and, indeed, more personalities needing to wake up and be introduced to Grace and to the safe place house. I expect this psychological healing process will continue, at a measured pace, for the remainder of Grace's life.

Physical Healing

*G*race had just switched with one of her personalities; allowing a child personality--perhaps age five or six--to take control over her body. She was enjoying being "out" and started running about in our front yard. I watched in satisfaction since this demonstration of joy was a sign of my wife's progress in her healing. Happiness had been a rare emotion for Grace's personalities. They contained the bulk of the horrific memories of abuse and, generally, emerged from Grace's subconscious mind with much fear and sorrow. Only after considerable psychological healing progress would a personality be free enough from the abusive memories to be joyful. After ten minutes or so of this fun, the child personality switched "back into" my wife's subconscious mind and my wife reappeared. She immediately began gasping for breath and collapsed on the grass. Anxiously, I ran over to her ready to give assistance. Between gasps of breath, she told me that her heart was pounding from the exertion of running about. Her older body was completely exhausted.

This describes one of the strangest effects of Grace's multiple personality disorder: the effective age of her body appeared to depend on which personality was in control. When a child personality was "out," her body functioned with the stamina and energy appropriate for the child's age. As soon as Grace switched back and took control of her body, the body functioned with the stamina and energy of an adult's body and, in this example, was exhausted from the exertions of the younger child. This incident exemplifies some of the extreme physical problems that my wife encountered during her healing.

1. Signs

A common and, frankly, disgusting physical sign of satanic abuse is missing or damaged genital organs. Grace was no exception to this sign. She was missing an ovary. Her conscious memory was that her ovary contained a bleeding cyst and required removal when she was a young teenager. However, her subconscious memories indicated a different reason for losing her ovary. That reason was the retaliation for her decision to become a Christian.

A second and frequent physical harbinger of Grace's abuse was biting her tongue. I occasionally have experienced this brief but painful sensation of biting my tongue or the inside of my mouth while eating. But it happens infrequently for me, maybe several times a year; whereas for my wife this can be a weekly or sometimes even a daily occurrence. Grace's tongue biting seems to be caused by two factors. First, if a personality even partially switches out during eating, jaw motion becomes uncoordinated resulting in the tongue biting. Also, personalities sometimes express their displeasure with my wife by causing her pain via tongue biting. Whatever the cause, the tongue biting has been a consistent but minor irritant for my wife and a sign of deeper issues needing attention.

The psychological healing accomplished by my wife was centered on undoing the cult programming and processing the abusive memories. These efforts involved the release of intense feelings and memories mostly resident in her subconscious personality states. Her memories of the abuse were intimately coupled with her physical body. In many cases even though the abuse and injury to her body occurred many years ago, the remembered memories triggered painful physical responses requiring treatment in the present. In this chapter, I will describe

Physical Healing

the efforts that have enabled my wife to heal physically from the trauma caused by her extreme childhood abuse.

In addition to the physical memory healing, there were a number of physical issues caused in Grace's present by the psychological healing and the personality multiplicity. For example, the intense stress and anxiety caused by the released memories triggered much depression. The depression was a severe issue requiring immediate medical attention. Also, the multiplicity raised a number of unusual health issues such as a child personality's affect on an older body as described at the beginning of this chapter. Preventing health issues when new personalities emerged required careful attention and planning. These physical healing issues will also be described in this chapter.

2. Body Memories

As a child and adolescent, Grace dissociated the feelings generated by the abuse she suffered. Her dissociation was extreme causing the multiple personality disorder. Much of the abuse was extremely painful so many of these stored feelings were centered on the pain. Eventually the dissociation began "breaking down" and some of the stored feelings began "leaking out." Furthermore, as the psychological healing progressed the hidden feelings were further accessed and released. The mind and body are so intimately connected that, as the feelings were released, Grace relived aspects of the abuse a second time. It was as if past abusive injuries were manifested in the present to be healed. I will give several examples of this.

The first example is that of horrific retaliatory abuse suffered by Grace for becoming a Christian. In her early teens Grace made the decision to become a Christian. Not surprisingly, this decision evoked extreme, life threatening retaliation. The retaliation was carried out by her father and a physician in a hospital room. As a young teen, Grace had chronic problems with cysts on her ovaries. During one of these episodes, she was admitted to the hospital. There she was taken to a room with her father, a physician and a nurse. The nurse was ordered out of the room and the two men began the purposeful and painful damaging of her ovaries. They did this by beating on her abdomen and pulling internally on her reproductive organs. The excessive pain rendered her unconscious and she, eventually, woke up in another hospital room having undergone surgery for the removal of an ovary. She remembers the doctor who had done the surgery telling her that the surgical staff was surprised at the torn and bleeding condition of her ovary upon removal. Years later when checking for evidence of this abuse she was told that all medical records of this operation were missing.

This abuse had two significant effects on Grace. First and foremost, she has never been able to bear children. This was simply a consequence of making a decision that eventually would cause her to leave the cult. Any such decision has extreme and life-long consequences. Secondly, the painful feelings generated by this abuse were so intense that they could not be effectively stored in Grace's subconscious mind and would often "leak out." Throughout most of our marriage, Grace has had consistent pain in her abdomen. On a monthly basis it would plague her. This pain, although generated by a memory, was very real to Grace. There seemed to be no solution until these memories were released through the psychological healing. For many years now Grace has been relatively pain free in her abdominal area. This physical healing was a direct result of the psychological healing.

As has been previously mentioned in other chapters, Grace was used as a "breeder" for the delivery of babies to be sacrificed in cult rituals. Not surprisingly such activity generated horrific memories that required many personalities for storage. In one pregnancy, the baby was prematurely pulled out of Grace's womb by her father resulting in hemorrhaging. This was a life threatening situation for Grace and a life ending experience for her child. Containing these memories required three adolescent personalities. During the psychological healing stage these three personalities emerged along with all the horrific feelings and infirmity caused by the event. Grace's body essentially relived the effects of the abuse. Fortunately, these personalities emerged and consciously controlled Grace's body for only short periods of time over several years. This effectively diluted the effects of this memory on Grace's body. Between the switching out times, the three personalities rested in Grace's safe place house recuperating. After many years of healing, these personalities are completely healthy and are in the process of merging with Grace.

The psychological healing of Grace's personalities who experienced child birthing was traumatic for both Grace and me. As these personalities emerged from Grace's unconscious mind so did their feelings and experiences. As a young adolescent, Grace's body was not given the time for processing and healing from the birthing process. This need for physical healing remained latent in the personality states storing this information. Thus, as these personalities emerged the opportunity for finally processing these body feelings emerged as well. I will never forget my utter amazement in seeing my wife's body writhe in labor pains when one of these personalities emerged. There was little I could do but watch and speak encouragement. Eventually this episode stopped as Grace's body processed through these labor pains and experiences from the past. Once completed these labor pain echoes never reoccurred. Grace's body had finally healed from the child birthing experienced as a young adolescent.

As Grace's healing progressed many personalities emerged containing other memories of the physical abuse. In many instances, these memories caused Grace real pain in the present when her body responded as if the abuse had just occurred. Again my interpretation of this is that the effects of the abuse had not been fully processed and experienced as a child but were rather stored in Grace's subconscious mind. Now, many years later, these stored feelings were accessed via the psychological healing and were given the opportunity to be fully processed and felt. A good example of this involves a bite from a poisonous spider. One of the activities Grace was forced to participate in as a child was putting her hand into a box containing poisonous spiders, probably black widow spiders. Apparently in one such instance Grace was bitten by a spider. The corresponding feelings were dissociated and, hence, stored in her subconscious mind. Now many years later these feeling were accessed when the personality containing this memory emerged. This memory not only caused Grace's body acute pain but irritation and swelling of the skin on her hand. Grace immediately applied a soothing cream to her hand and treated it as if the spider bite had just occurred. Eventually, the swelling and irritation subsided. Her hand was healed physically and the memory was fully processed.

3   Multiplicity Effects

In a very real sense, I have learned how the physical body is "driven" by the conscious mind. This has been very evident when Grace's younger personalities have emerged. The example at the beginning of this chapter is a good illustration of this effect. The child personality that took control of Grace's body in this example effectively "drove" the adult body as if it were only five or six years old. The activity and energy levels of Grace's body responded as if the body was only five or six years old; matching the age of the conscious mind controlling it at the time. This seems ridiculous based on the medical science I am familiar with; but I have witnessed this effect many times.

Although this effect seems benign, much caution must be taken because of it. For example, what if a child personality was out when Grace took her medication? Would Grace's childlike body be over dosed with an adult's medication dose? One of Grace's therapists knew of such a situation resulting in a lengthy coma when a child personality ingested an adult dose of medicine. To prevent this, we established a basic rule that only Boss Grace, the adult personality, be out and in control of the body when medication was being taken.

My wife's multiplicity frequently caused dis-coordination in her body. Although not serious, this effect could be irritating. It was most evident when Grace was eating. If a personality even partially emerged during this time, the moment of confused control over the body would likely result in inadvertent but painful tongue biting. During the height of Grace's healing process, she would bite her tongue several times a week or sometimes even daily. This problem was further aggravated by the actions of some personalities. Sometimes to get attention or to express disapproval they would come out briefly, bite the tongue and then retreat to the subconscious mind avoiding the pain. To counter this, we established a rule of feeling the pain when a personality was "out." This rule was still not entirely successful since the personalities prone to such mouth biting activity typically were new emerging personalities and were unaware of the rules. Fortunately as Grace's healing has progressed, this minor but unsettling mouth biting issue has significantly reduced in its frequency of occurrence.

Another effect of the dis-coordination caused by switching personalities was clumsiness. For example, I have seen Grace literally trip over her own feet while walking. Initially perplexed by this seemingly clumsy gait, I now realize that a personality switch caused this seemingly dis-coordination. Other examples include dropping items in her hand and miscalculating the distance to objects. Since most of Grace's personality states are little girls, the perception of distance with a larger adult body was different. Thus, when these personalities were controlling the body there was a tendency for miscalculating distances and bumping the head on a shelf or car door etc. All of these effects are minor irritants that Grace has learned to live with.

4. Depression

Remembering the extreme childhood abuse understandably caused Grace much sorrow, stress and anxiety. These factors all contributed to depression that became suicidal for her. Countering this depression, Grace's psychiatrists prescribed anti-depressant drugs. These drugs reduced Grace's depression giving her a better quality of life while going through the healing process. The medication also enabled Grace to put energy and time into the healing process rather than into fighting the depression. The prescription drugs were absolutely vital for Grace's healing and deprogramming. Without these prescription drugs, I have no doubt that Grace would have committed suicide. The drug therapy effectively saved her life. However, one detrimental side effect of this medication was weight gain. Now after the completion of the bulk of the healing, Grace has been left with the legacy of excessive body fat. Grace's weight gain is not entirely due to the drug therapy alone. As a child, Grace was virtually force fed to gain weight. The extra weight as a child effectively hid her pregnancies. In either case, the excessive weight is problematic and Grace struggles today with related health issues.

5. Preventative Measures

In several instances, Grace used physical actions as preventative measures. For example, a frequent cult ritual was the marking of flesh by cutting shapes and symbols into the skin of a victim. Such cutting evoked much pain but would also heal provided the cuts were paper-like shallow cuts. Such experiences as a child generated psychological echoes in the present for Grace and often she found herself suppressing the desire to cut her own skin. This desire was amplified if she saw kitchen knives setting on a table or counter top. When these urges became strong she used a technique learned from the hospital staff during a hospital stay. She simply placed ice on the body location of the desired cutting, typically her arms. This harmless inducement of pain became a substitute for the potential pain that would be caused by cutting herself.

In several instances, Grace also used physical action for diverting a greater remembered or emotional pain with a lesser but immediate physical pain. A not so harmless example of pain diversion was head banging. Often I have stopped Grace from pummeling her head with her fists as hard as she could. The reason for doing this was generating a minor pain to divert the greater pain of remembered abuse.

Suicide was always a very real threat for Grace. The agony of remembering the horrible abuse, much of it caused or allowed by her parents, was often overwhelming for her. Suicide then became a possible escape for one so familiar with death anyway. Fortunately, Grace was able to resist this temptation repeatedly but there were several "close calls." In one of these, Grace was tempted to go into the kitchen and use the kitchen knives to slash her wrists. She averted this temptation by taking the physical action of sitting on her hands in another room. Later on, since I was at work at the time, she told me that she sat on her hands for two or three hours before the suicidal urge left.

6. Key Lessons

The most surprising learning during Grace's extreme healing process was the powerful effect of Grace's mind on her physical body. I found that the remembered pain episodes were "mind boggling." The painful feelings inflicted on Grace as a child apparently laid dormant for decades in her subconscious mind and then manifested with almost full force when accessed in the healing process. Similarly, when new personalities "switched out" into Grace's conscious mind the effect on Grace's body was also profound. As described in this chapter, the physiology of Grace's body was determined mainly by the age of the personality controlling the body. I suspect that medical practitioners would deny this possibility but I have experienced this startling effect with Grace.

7. Summary

Grace's physical healing included two key components. The first component is the physical healing from the remembered abuse from her childhood. Most if not all of this physical healing has been accomplished. Nearly all memories of the extreme abuse Grace suffered as a child have been released. Grace has been freed from her abusive past.

The second component involves healing from the psychological healing process itself. For example, the legacy for Grace generated by taking a multitude of medications during the healing process has been weight gain. In addition, just the sheer exhaustion of a decade of extreme healing has left Grace chronically fatigued. It is likely that she will suffer from these physical issues for the remainder of her life. But these physical issues are an acceptable penalty for all the other spiritual and psychological healing accomplished by Grace. Grace is now free from the abuse and satanic cult bondage suffered as a child.

Challenges

My wife's extreme healing has been a tremendous challenge for both Grace and me as well as for the members of her healing team. For Grace, the challenge has been to fight for her mind and life. She has succeeded. The deprogramming and spiritual exorcism has been accomplished and Grace has wrestled control of her subconscious mind away from the cults and their implanted demon cohorts. Physically she has resisted the urges for suicide and has circumvented all the personality suicide traps set by the cult. My challenge has been managing the healing process, learning how to help Grace, implementing that learning and continuing the struggle until completion. The necessary knowledge for this was learned mainly through trial and error, from medical team members and by guidance from the Holy Spirit. Implementing this knowledge over a decade of healing has required persistence and just plain stubbornness in refusing to give up; especially for me since I always had the option of just "walking away" and living my life without these challenges of extreme healing. The challenge for Grace's healing team has been patience and discerning how to best help Grace and myself. Being a problem solver, I understand the intense desire to just tell someone how to solve an issue. I suspect that members of the healing team, especially the therapists, often had the same urge but instead were patience in exerting their professional care for Grace. For much of Grace's healing was accomplished by enabling her, not telling her, how to figure out the best solutions for the many issues she faced.

My wife and I have triumphed over the challenge of extreme healing. Based on our success, I extend various aspects of this challenge to others. In general, I challenge the victims of abuse, especially victims of satanic ritual abuse, and their spouses to engage in the healing process and persist in it until completed. I also challenge medical professionals and therapists to continue their essential work in helping victims heal. I challenge pastors, priests and spiritual professionals as well as Christians in general to become more involved in the healing work for victims, especially for those victims of satanic ritual abuse. Finally, I challenge the general public to accept the possibility that this extreme abuse goes on in our midst.

More specifically, I challenge the abuse victim to get the necessary psychotherapy and then continue with that therapy until all issues are resolved. If the abuse is extreme, by all means get spiritual counseling as well. Make sure that you have the spiritual covering of your spouse and a pastor, priest or spiritual leader. If you are not sure if you are an abuse victim but have persistent nightmares or emotional outbursts that are out of proportion to a stimulus, check it out. Talk to a therapist and investigate the origins of these issues. Life is meant to be enjoyed and the effects of abuse simply fester and hinder the joy in life. They will not "go away" if unattended. Although the effort required was tremendous, my wife's healing has given her much improved quality of life now and likely will yield eternal benefits. If she was able to go through the extreme healing required for her incredible, life threatening satanic ritual abuse, I think that anybody can go through the effort required for the healing from their abuse, whatever that abuse may be.

Next, I challenge the spouses of abuse victims to persist in their partner's struggle for healing. Do not succumb to the temptation of leading a happier life by simply walking away

Challenges

from the tremendous problems your partner is facing. Instead do what is right and support your partner. For the extreme case of satanic ritual abuse, I especially challenge spouses to join your partner in the fight for freedom from cult mind control and healing from cult abuse. This is a battle waged far more successfully when couples are fully engaged together. It will be a long and arduous battle but it can be won. Our successful battle overcoming satanic cult control and abuse in Grace's life is proof of this.

The general challenge of joining your partner in the healing battle has more specific ramifications, especially for extreme healing. Spouses of abuse victims must learn, implement and manage the tools and resources needed for healing. This book can be used as a guide for this. But be aware that your partner's healing process may be quite different in many aspects from Grace's healing due to different individual characteristics. Hopefully, the principles listed in the Themes chapter are general enough for application to most cases of extreme healing and, therefore, useful for guidance.

The key healing tools Grace and I utilized for her healing were the spiritual, psychological and emotional orientated tools described in this book. I found that learning, implementing and managing these tools was a challenge, but a challenge I overcame. Accordingly, I pass this challenge on to other spouses that find themselves in a similar situation; needing to help their spouse heal from abuse.

The first such tool is providing the spiritual covering for your partner. The Holy Spirit will help you fulfill this important role. Do not shy away from the responsibilities of this role such as the spiritual exorcism of demons. Although doing this can be spooky at times, I found it to be the easiest part of the extreme healing. I learned to say the phase "in the name of the Lord Jesus Christ" really fast and quickly mastered the tools of deep level spiritual warfare that were needed.

An important resource for healing is the team of medical and spiritual professionals as well as friends willing to help. The spouse must first set up this team and then manage the interaction with this team. This includes managing the financing necessary to pay for medical and therapeutic services. Accordingly, the challenge is for spouses to be totally engaged in the healing process of their partner by managing the "logistics" of the healing process and providing the necessary funds for the healing process. I also challenge spouses to refrain from problem solving and, instead, engage in listening carefully to your partner. In my experience, nine times out of ten the solution to a particular abuse issue came from Grace herself. I just provided a "sounding board" enabling her to verbalize her thoughts and, thus, formulate solutions for the issue under consideration. Encouragement is a general enabling tool of life. But it is even more important as the healing becomes more difficult. Many times Grace was on the verge of "giving up" and needed encouragement to continue the healing efforts. Therapists know the value of encouragement and are great encouragers. But the day to day encouragement duties fall to the spouse. Finally, I challenge the spouse to be considerate and patient with your partner. These tools of love are essential to marriage and become even more important during the healing process. There will be an end to the stress of the healing battle and life will return almost back to normal. But in the meantime, implementing the tools of a loving relationship is even more important for the marriage as well as for healing success.

My main challenge for medical professionals is to keep up the good work. I have been impressed with the high quality of assistance Grace has received from her psychotherapists and from her psychiatrists. I have no doubt that without your help Grace would now be either dead or psychotic. I do extend one challenge to therapists, especially to non Christian therapists. Please consider the spiritual component involved in the abuse, especially for satanic ritual abuse, and advise the abuse victim to get spiritual help from a Christian pastor or priest. The psychological healing will be limited unless there is concurrent spiritual healing.

My challenge for the pastor, priest or spiritual leader is to be prepared and alert for those victims of satanic ritual abuse in your congregation or parish. If your leadership extends over several hundred persons, it is likely that there will be such a person in attendance. These victims and their families need the spiritual covering and support that only you can provide. Also be aware when your counseling training and abilities are being exceeded. Provide only spiritual help for the victim of satanic ritual abuse. The psychological counsel necessary for helping victims of satanic ritual abuse requires specialized training and experience that even most licensed therapists do not have. Instead advise the victim to seek psychotherapy. At the earliest stage of healing, Grace got counseling from the pastor of the church we were attending. He had the great foresight and wisdom after several counseling sessions to suggest that Grace seek advice from a professional therapist. Had he continued with his counseling it would have been not only a waste of his time but also could have been damaging for Grace. I also challenge the pastor or priest to be specific and gentle in their interaction with victims. The "deep level" spiritual warfare that I have engaged in is very specific. General prayers give the enemy loopholes that can be turned to their advantage. For example, do not pray in the name of Jesus but rather in the name of Jesus Christ. This concept of specificity was described in the Spiritual Healing chapter. Also be gentle in your prayers. Loud prayers can be interpreted as abusive by victims since it will remind them of the violence associated with the abuse. Remember that the name of Jesus Christ contains so much power and authority that it simply needs to be whispered to be effective.

For Christians I have several challenges. First, I challenge Christians to not shun victims of satanic ritual abuse. Grace and I have experienced this behavior so many times that we no longer tell our friends anything about Grace's past. We have had many friends that purposely withdrew from our friendship and avoided spending time with us upon understanding Grace's background and issues. Of course this was the opposite of what Grace really needed. Friendship is especially valuable when one is going through great stresses in life. I have also witnessed the negative effects of spurned friendship on our friends themselves. For when a choice was made to avoid Grace, I think that choice became an affront to the Holy Spirit. For the Holy Spirit had done so much work in Grace that a decision to avoid Grace effectively became a decision to avoid His work done in her. Of course the Holy Spirit is not vindictive but I think that when people purposely reject His workings they are effectively rejecting Him. I suspect that such decisions open the doors for attack by the enemy.

Instead of shunning and avoiding victims of satanic ritual abuse, I challenge Christians to engage in the battle against Satan and his kingdom. Form spiritual warfare teams to help and befriend the victims of abuse. Any form of abuse represents the work of Satan's kingdom. But sooner or later those victims seeking help will include those abused directly by Satan and his demonic hordes. As mentioned previously, I believe that for the first time in history all the tools for helping victims of satanic ritual abuse are available. Not coincidentally, I also believe that Satan and his deeds are being revealed as the end of this age approaches. I suspect that an era of healing from satanic ritual abuse is beginning. This healing is a consequence of revealing Satan's kingdom that will lead, in part, to the destruction of his kingdom. What an exciting

Challenges

time to live. Christians please join Grace and myself in the battle against Satan's kingdom. Grace's survival and extreme healing is proof that the battle can be won now.

www.ingramcontent.com/pod-product-compliance
Lightning Source LLC
Chambersburg PA
CBHW061643040426
42446CB00010B/1553